Chasing
John Byng

A Tour Into Lincolnshire

Chasing
John Byng

A Tour Into Lincolnshire

JOHN TAYLOR

authority publishing.

First published in 2005 by Authority Publishing,
7 Coppice Hill, Bradford on Avon, Wiltshire BA15 1JT
www.authoritypublishing.co.uk
Authority Publishing is a member of the Independent Publishers Guild.

A catalogue record for this book is available from the British Library.

ISBN 0-9551288-1-1

Design by PawPrint
Set in Century Schoolbook

Printed in the UK by Cambrian Printers, Aberystwyth, North Wales

For Victoria

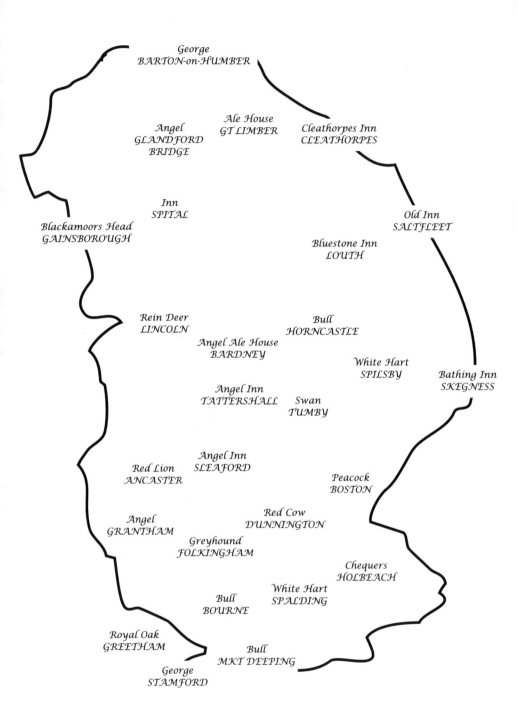

George
BARTON-on-HUMBER

Ale House
GT LIMBER

Angel
GLANDFORD
BRIDGE

Cleathorpes Inn
CLEATHORPES

Inn
SPITAL

Old Inn
SALTFLEET

Blackamoors Head
GAINSBOROUGH

Bluestone Inn
LOUTH

Rein Deer
LINCOLN

Bull
HORNCASTLE

Angel Ale House
BARDNEY

White Hart
SPILSBY

Angel Inn
TATTERSHALL

Swan
TUMBY

Bathing Inn
SKEGNESS

Angel Inn
SLEAFORD

Red Lion
ANCASTER

Peacock
BOSTON

Angel
GRANTHAM

Red Cow
DUNNINGTON

Greyhound
FOLKINGHAM

Chequers
HOLBEACH

White Hart
SPALDING

Bull
BOURNE

Royal Oak
GREETHAM

Bull
MKT DEEPING

George
STAMFORD

JOHN BYNG: A Tour Into Lincolnshire 1791

	Day	Night
23rd June		Bull, Market Deeping
24th June	Bull, Bourne	Greyhound, Folkingham
25th June		"
26th June		Angel Inn, Sleaford
27th June		"
28th June		Rein Deer, Lincoln
29th June		"
30th June	Angel Ale House, Bardney	Swan, Tumby
1st July		"
2nd July	Angel Inn, Tattershall	Angel Inn, Sleaford
3rd July	Red Cow, Dunnington	White Hart, Spalding
4th July		"
5th July	Chequers, Holbeach	Peacock, Boston
6th July		White Hart, Spilsby
7th July	Bathing Inn, Skegness	"
8th July		Bull, Horncastle
9th July		Bluestone Inn, Louth
10th July		"
11th July	Old Inn, Saltfleet	Cleathorpes Inn
12th July	Ale House, Great Limber	George, Barton-on-Humber
13th July	Angel, Glandford Bridge	Inn, Spital
14th July	Blackamoors Head, Gainsborough	Rein Deer, Lincoln
15th July		"
16th July	Red Lion, Ancaster	Angel, Grantham
17th July	Royal Oak, Greetham (Rutland)	George, Stamford

CONTENTS

When first Imagination fills the Mind,
And Hope delusive leaves slow doubt behind
The eager Tourist hastens to begin
His fancied Journey to a pleasant Inn;
Where many a Traveller in days of old
Has trod good Roads, and good Adventures told;

The Prospects fine and the Horizon gay
Speaks lucky Weather; and a prosp'rous day;
Till at the close of Eve, benumb'd, bemired,
Himself wet thro', and Rosinante tired,
At a cold Inn, without a pitying Friend,
Obliged to tarry and his cash to spend,
Repentance comes on fast; — And far from home,
He strangely wonders what could make him roam.

JOHN BYNG

This Byng thing

'W
ho is this Bling and what's he done to annoy you?" My wife could put up with my chunterings no longer.

"I'm not annoyed," I snapped back, "and it's not Bling. It's Byng. BYNG!"

"Okay, Bing-Bing. Who's he?"

"Not Bing-Bing. You make him sound like a gift from the Chinese government to bolster the world's panda population. His name's John Byng and he's a diarist. Or rather he was. He died in 1813."

"You're annoyed with a guy who's been dead for two hundred years? It can't have been anything personal."

Faced with such impeccable wifely logic, I calmed a little. "He wrote this book, *Rides Round Britain*, that they sent me from the book club."

"And it's not very good?"

"It's brilliant. It's a reprint of the tours Byng made on horseback in the eighteenth century, staying at inns and writing about his experiences. There's a Tour Into Sussex; a Tour Into Kent; a Tour Into Wales..."

"But?"

"But there's no Tour Into Lincolnshire."

"Maybe he didn't have time."

"That's the whole point. Not only did he have time, he

actually made a Tour Into Lincolnshire. It's here on page 273."

"Make up your mind. Is it in there or isn't it?"

"It's a footnote, a piffling footnote. Look." I made a stabbing gesture at the middle of the guilty page as I passed the volume over.

She read aloud with exaggerated lack of interest: *'Tour To The North 1792: My chestnut mare Spot, who is in fine order, I shall ride from town and, when at Biggleswade, shall take up my bay gelding Bumper for the carriage of Garwood and our baggage...'* Well?"

"Well, who is Garwood?"

"How the hell do I know? It's your obsession."

"Look at the footnote — at the bottom of the page."

"I know where to find a footnote, thank you!" Her turn to snap as she squinted to take in the tiny print: "Garwood: Byng's new valet, taken on for his tour of Lincolnshire in June 1791."

"Exactly!" I claimed my victory with a sharp nod of the head and a note of triumph in my voice. After a pause for breath, I resumed my rant: "It just really annoys me that everything to do with Lincolnshire is considered expendable, or boring, or as some kind of music hall joke. Book's overrun. Don't worry — take out the chapter about Lincolnshire. No one will notice.

"They just miss the point, these people," I continued at fever pitch. "The great thing about Lincolnshire is that nothing happens and nobody goes there. That's how it keeps its beauty. It must be more interesting than Biggleswade, for God's sake. Anyway, subject closed. I won't mention it again."

But she knew that I would. Knew that it would become a quest: to track down that missing Tour Into Lincolnshire; to find out whatever became of all those coaching inns; maybe

4

even to go back to our native county after ten years of living abroad and look at it through a traveller's eyes; through John Byng's eyes...

John Byng was not worried about others' views of his writing. *'I dread not the reviewers as I shall never hazard a bookseller's window; for the grocer do I waste so much white paper.'* The fact that my own efforts have reached publication stage is due entirely to the support of my wife Victoria as travelling companion, critic and helper. Even then, I might not have ventured into print had I not happened across artist Diane Brookes at the Alford Craft Market. My request for illustrations "that look as if they were drawn by someone on a horse" obviously did not faze her!

In my researches, I have had considerable help from the staff of all of the Lincolnshire libraries, particularly at Lincoln where the Byng manuscript is housed.

My thanks to Paul Gent, for acting as editor, Keith Horsewood and David Penman. The unusual spellings in Byng's quotations are as he wrote them. Any others are my own work.

The Greyhound, Folkingham

24ᴛʜ Jᴜɴᴇ 1791 *The prettily-placed town of Folkingham, upon a rising ground, soon appear'd in sight, with its grand new inn at the top of the market-place; an inn worthy of the Bath road but here sees not two post chaises in a day. The trustees of Sir Gilbert Heathcote having bought this estate are nobly laying out its annual produce upon new buildings in this town and have already expended £4000 upon this inn, without raising the rent. After a long talk with the landlord (who is of the Spanish kind, proud and lolling in his chair) and having seen his great kitchen and superb range, I walk'd around the mounds of the old castle.*

Bill for 2 nights: £1 1s 3d *This bill is as reasonable as can be and unless the inn should not find better customers than myself it must be quickly undone.*

Quickly undone

Market Deeping — Bourne — Folkingham

The horse was sturdy but smaller and less well-bred than expected, thought the ostler as he held on to the dusty steed's reins and let the gentleman dismount. For gentleman he certainly was, and it was this that made him unusual. Though Lincolnshire in the Year of our Lord Seventeen Hundred and Ninety-One was undoubtedly a backwater, the Bull at Market Deeping had still welcomed its fair share of toffs and aristocracy. But they came by mail coach or more often in their own phaetons or post-chaises, expecting a change of horse at all hours of the night, shouting their orders and treating as stupid an experienced stablehand who knew better than they did how to look after their animals.

But this gentleman was riding alone, if you didn't count the equally dusty panting dog which refused to leave his side, and moreover was courteous and patient. He must be a military man, the ostler had decided when he first spotted him from the bar room's tiny bow window that jutted out into the inn yard and made steering a coach through the battered semi-circular topped archway just that little more difficult. Yes, a man used to the saddle and to his own company.

Colonel John Byng had indeed been a soldier for more than 20 years, rising to Lieutenant-Colonel in the 1st Foot Guards. But that had ended some 11 years before when adventure had given way to a monotonous desk job at the Inland Revenue at Somerset House. It was as a tourist that he now arrived, somewhat reluctantly, in front of the low, yellow-grey stone inn. That morning he had sent on ahead his man-servant Garwood with luggage and instructions to secure the best room available. But he knew that even the finest chamber at this mean and dirty house would not stand comparison with his lodgings of the night before. He had discovered the almost perfect inn at Wansford on the Great North Road at about the same time as he had decided to relieve the tedium of his desk-bound job by planning and undertaking an annual tour and keeping a written and pictorial record of his travels around Britain.

Though he had no ambition for his diaries to be published in his lifetime, Byng's Tour Into Lincolnshire would be his eleventh. It was the idea of his friend and travelling companion Colonel Bertie who, as a relation of the Earls of Lindsey, was connected to many of the great and the good of the county. But, 13 days after leaving home in London, there was still no sign of Bertie and no news of when he might arrive, though he had sent along his "immovably stupid" dog Ranger for company.

Having dismounted and handed the animals over to the ostler and to Garwood, Byng took advantage of the warm June evening to stroll by the river and into the churchyard, before returning to the Bull at nine o'clock to take his supper with wine. He ordered a half pint of brandy and retired early to bed to write up his diary:

'I left Wansford at 4 o'clock in a very fine evening and arrived at seven o'clock at Market Deeping, a mean long town. Till nine o'clock I wander'd about by the river side and into the church-yard, my old stroule. This is a very low, damp situation and the natives appear Flemish in their looks and the length of their round hair. As for my landlord, he was

civil but his red wind was not drinkable. I supp'd at nine o'clock and retired early to bed, after having gone over the Stamford news paper. Peterborough Races ended yesterday; all the quality of this place return'd in the evening much satisfied with the last day's sport. My bed room was cold and miserable with an horrid putridity of blankets, over which I prudently pour'd part of my half pint of brandy as I have often done in Wales.'

'So why are we in a sports car?" My wife's sudden question distracted me and I almost missed the last parking place in the market square in Deeping, just wide enough to ensure no scratches on the left-hand drive BMW Z3 Roadster, my pride and joy.

"What do you mean?" I enquired, though I had a fair idea what was coming next.

"Well," she continued as I applied the handbrake and switched off the engine, "if we're recreating John Byng's tour of Lincolnshire of 1791, why aren't we on horseback?"

"Firstly, he used the transport of his day and so shall we. Secondly, none of the inns we'll be staying at has stabling and, thirdly and most importantly, I can't ride a horse."

"Good publicity, though?"

"It would certainly make the newspapers when we were run down by a 38-tonne truck on the Spalding by-pass."

We ducked under the low front door of the Bull and made our way into The Dugout, the oldest part of the pub, where I ordered drinks and sandwiches with a portion of chips for luck and the inquisition continued.

"Are there any similarities?"

"Byng arrived in Lincolnshire on June the 23rd. Today's June the 23rd. He was called John; I'm called John. He was 47; I'm 47 — is that enough?"

"Was he grumpy, too?"

"He disliked injustice, cruelty, social pretences, pine trees, landscape gardeners, absentee landlords, bad food, slovenly inns, the French..."

"I'll take that as a yes, then. Where was Mrs Byng when her old man was off on his tours?"

"Back home in London looking after the children — they had 13 — and shopping in Bond Street. Oh, and she was having an affair with one of his friends."

"So I'm just here as insurance?"

"No. You're my travelling companion. Byng had 'Col B'; you can be 'Mrs T' — unless you see yourself more as Garwood, carrying the bags, serving the meals, dressing me..."

"Travelling companion sounds fine. What are the rules?"

"In three weeks, Byng had lunch or stayed the night at 27 inns. According to my research, there are 15 still in existence. If they serve drinks, we have a drink; if they do food, we eat there, non-meat options permitting; and if they have accommodation, we stay the night. In the meantime, we follow Byng's route and take in some of the sights that he saw, plus a few new ones. And by the end of eight days we should know whether Lincolnshire really is a cultural and gastronomic desert, or if it's just had a bad press. Deal?" I offered my outstretched hand and we shook on it.

"It's a deal. So what do we do now?"

"Sit back, listen and observe. We're diarists, remember."

Byng had found the natives Flemish in their appearance. In the Year of Our Lord Two Thousand and Three, they seemed a very cosmopolitan crowd, public school accents mixing with a Fenland burr that owed more to Norfolk than Lincolnshire dialect. Topics deemed fit for discussion proved very catholic, too — sailing boats, the desert camel train and the best route from the Deepings to the Ascot Races. There's a strange kind of protocol to pub chatter that I had forgotten in my ten years living in Monaco. Each participant looks totally bored by the other's chosen topic — probably having heard it a thousand times before. Bored, but not resentful; merely biding his time until his turn comes around and with it his chance to spout forth to an uninterested audience.

The Bull no longer offers accommodation or evening meals, but it is everything an English pub should be. A cheerful and attentive landlord; a sunny beer garden; clean loos and good food.

"This house wine is very good," said Mrs T with a half-smile. "Make a note of that. Red *wind* very drinkable."

She had read the original tour after all.

Byng left early from Market Deeping. *'From the altogether of last night, I find myself very unwell today and my throat very sore. I go in search of better quarters.'*

A brief note in his diaries shows he stopped at Bourne for lunch. *'This inn, another Bull, is not so dirty as the Deeping Bull but full as ill-managed, with a waiter of long black hair and low'ring shaggy eyebrows.'*

"You'll like the next one," I promised Mrs T, showing her a photo of a magnificent Edwardian Tudor building with four dormer windows overlooking Bourne town centre. "It's the birthplace of the illustrious Elizabethan statesman William Cecil, later Lord Burghley, trusted advisor to Queen Elizabeth I," I quoted from my research.

After rising to become the Queen's chief minister, Cecil had built himself a far grander edifice, Burghley House near Stamford. His childhood home ceased to be a private residence as far back as 1717 when it was known as the Bull and Swan, later just the Bull and, following extensive renovation in 1955, renamed the Burghley Arms.

It was sunny enough to leave the roof down as we parked the BMW by the basking ducks in Bourne's beautiful park and strolled up to admire the Burghley Arms' magnificent architecture and gaily-coloured display of hanging baskets.

Inside, deafening noise greeted us from the back bar. George Michael at his glass-shattering loudest was blasting out his greatest hits for the benefit of a handful of bikers and assorted locals. In the front lounge, where once Cecil had dreamed of greatness, two youths were discussing the previous night's sexual encounters, real or imagined. The door to the ladies toilet showed the scars of having been kicked in and the foam stuffing of the plush seats burst out through gaping slash wounds.

"Do you serve food at lunchtimes?" I yelled at the barmaid over a crescendo of *Careless Whisper*.

"Nah," she barked back.

"Just at night?"

"Nah."

"Well, two pints of Guinness and a packet of salted peanuts then, please."

"Nah sal'ed. Onny dry roast."

"That'll be fine."

So we sat in a corner, gazing at the magnificent pair of stone mullioned windows — each with six leaded lights — and sadly shaking our heads. If George Michael had stopped to draw breath for even a second, there would have been heard the sound of loud tutting.

With music still ringing in our ears, we went in search of peace and found it at Sempringham. Past Stow Green, the site of ancient fairs, and miles away from traffic down a long farm track with no electricity stands the Church of St Andrew, all that remains of a once bustling village. St Mary's Priory, home to the only English monastic order, the Gilbertines, was founded here in 1139 by Saint Gilbert whose remains lie under the church aisle.

Edward I banished Princess Gwenllian to the care of the

abbey when she was only 17 months old for fear that she might rally followers of her father Llewellyn, the last true-born Prince of Wales. In 1337, she died there after 54 years of virtual imprisonment and the site has become a magnet for Welsh pilgrims, "a tiny corner of an English field that is forever Wales". Vandals destroyed a small memorial and in 2001 a large new stone was erected in honour of Princess Gwenllian. Though no hammer or chisel has touched the stone since it was blasted from the quarry, it casts a shadow in the shape of a nun.

There are few sadder sights than a closed pub. Except perhaps a pub that's barred and bolted and has a 'To Whom It May Concern' notice pinned in several places to its peeling doors, offering a long list of last-known addresses and haunts of the previous tenants. Especially when that pub represents the first night of the trip of a lifetime — a quest — and particularly when you have driven all the way through France just to be there.

Once a thriving market town, the village of Folkingham is dominated by the red brick façade of the Greyhound Inn, with its quirky, moustache-shaped window lintels. Sir Gilbert Heathcote bought the estate in 1788 and set about turning the town into an important stopping-off point for coaches following the turnpike roads between London and Lincoln. He almost rebuilt the Greyhound in his enthusiasm, with a new arch for coaches to pass through to the stables and an assembly room which doubled as a courtroom for the Quarter Sessions after the town hall had been demolished.

It was in this pristine state that John Byng found it in 1791 and much enjoyed his stay. He rightly predicted its demise. But why now? Why tonight?

Just a year before, the Taylors had enjoyed a relaxing

lunchtime there in that modern rarity: a pub which offers good food yet welcomes dogs. We had spent the night at the nearby House of Correction, built in 1808 on the site of Folkingham Castle to put drunks and tramps back on the straight and narrow but restored in 1987 and rented out by the Landmark Trust to self-catering history buffs.

I knew of the inn's fascinating past from surfing the internet. I knew, too, that the "beautiful building now houses an antique and craft centre, a small friendly bar and restaurant of 30 covers and a garden centre in the summer season, as well as B & B rooms".

I was lacking only one vital piece of information: the Greyhound had closed suddenly the previous March. No wonder they hadn't answered my calls or replied to my fax.

Byng cleverly foresaw the undoing of the Greyhound: the place is far too grand for a village pub and was closed for many years during the late 20th century. But its latest closure is a further blow to a village desperately clinging to its identity. Quite simply, Folkingham with the Greyhound is an idyllic place. Without, it somehow loses its soul.

Perhaps in these days when discerning guests expect country houses that boast acres of garden, health complexes and sophisticated entertainment, the Greyhound's future as a hotel is bleak. But, as an architectural gem, surely it is worth preserving by one of the relevant charity organisations. With imagination, it could keep some form of licensed premises and restaurant — there is plenty of parking in the broad market square — but add meeting rooms and even a small theatre in the old ballroom.

I have long thought that there is no reason in rural communities why the doctor, the vicar, the policeman, the publican and the postmistress should not share premises to eliminate crippling building maintenance costs and better serve the community.

In another life, we might have inaugurated the Save the Greyhound Campaign, lobbied the local authority and stirred the villagers to action. But it was getting dark, we had nowhere to sleep and a new day's exploration was waiting for us.

30ᴛʜ JUNE 1791 *I accompanied a farmer who advised me to avoid Tattershall. I blunder'd my way to the little inn at Tumby where I was civilly receiv'd and lodg'd to my liking in the snug parlour of a thatch'd house, feeling myself in quiet and coolness after the noise and heat of the Lincoln inn. My supper (after many short walks) consisted of a fine roast fowl, cold ham, pickled salmon, artichoke and tarts, all in comfort, and I sat up till past eleven o'clock, writing and reading, for here were books!*

Bill for 1 night: 16s 8d *Breakfast 8d, Dinner 1s 6d, Supper 2s 6d, Coffee & tea 8d, Wine 3s, Punch etc 1s 6d, Servants eating & hay & corn 6s 10d. These little inns are pleasant pass-the-day spots but not so well at night when you want mattrasses and comforts.*

A tale of one city

Sleaford — Lincoln — Bardney — Coningsby

I t was the best of inns; it was the worst of inns. The Rein Deer at Lincoln brought out the best — and the worst — in Byng. He liked Lincoln a lot. His mood was lighter, his prose more flowery whenever he arrived in Lincolnshire's capital city. This was due in no small part to Lincoln Cathedral, *'the finest of our cathedrals I ever saw and why not, when rebuilding in London, follow such a model?'* Praise indeed.

And mostly he liked his lodgings, staying twice during his tour, alone for two nights and with his companion Colonel Bertie for a further two towards the end of his journeying.

On both occasions he toured the city's sights just as modern-day tourists follow in his footsteps. As well as the cathedral, where he attended a service and bemoaned the fact that so few were present, he also went to see the Roman Newport Arch and the ruins of both John of Gaunt's House and the old Bishop's Palace.

His first night at the inn was a big success: *'The Rein Deer, a large inn (at the foot of the hill and close to the Strong-Bow gate of Entrance to the Upper Town) receiv'd me hot and weary. Most eagerly did I seek my dinner and as eagerly drink of the very tolerable port wine.'*

By the second, his wanderings and the heat had left him a little frayed around the edges: *'I was tired and worn-down at my return when no strawberries could I get to cool my tongue! I had for my dinner two soles six inches long and a great, coarse duckling, the remembrance of which makes me sick.'*

By the end of his second stay he had decided firmly in favour of the Rein Deer. He paid his bill of £1 9s 1d (£1.45) for two nights and declared *'this is surely for a pompous inn in a great town a very cheap charge'.*

The French Revolution was unfolding during Byng's Tour Into Lincolnshire and at the Rein Deer he made clear his thoughts on that country and its ruler, Louis XVI: *'I read in the newspapers, with amazement, the accounts of the flight of the King of France; and of his capture, and being brought back: what a quick and wonderful retribution for his wanton assistance to our rebellious colonists whose flame of liberty has now so scorched him and his regal vanities. The pride and pomp of France consisted in her army, her clergy and her nobility; now debased, ejected and degraded. My opinion of France always was that they were 150 years behind this country in comforts, arts and science. Let them send here for a model of our constitution and not pretend to cobble one at home.'*

Having spent ten years living with the French, we couldn't help but remark that in the 21st century the boot was now firmly on the other foot. It is in England where services are crumbling and royalty fails in its duties, while in France the trains run on time, every village has its own transport and sports facilities, families still eat at table together and schools teach all children how to read and write.

It would have been nice to chew the cud on the state of Europe over a cold beer at the Rein Deer as Byng had done. But, sadly, it is no more, though there is a pub in the city which still bears the name. Byng's inn, once the Falcon, went through a whole host of further name changes —

including the George, the City Arms and the County Arms — before its license was withdrawn in 1922 and it was taken over by the Midland Bank.

The current building, with a magnificent painted ceiling, now houses the Lincoln branch of HSBC, though it is easy to imagine its illustrious past as an inn. The bank is right in the heart of the city's pedestrian shopping precinct and taking a photograph was proving difficult — until Mrs T had a brainwave. She clutched her clipboard to her bosom, held her pencil poised in anticipatory mood and made as if to stop innocent passers-by to garner their views on everything from double glazing to their favourite mayonnaise. A huge gap appeared in the crowds as embarrassed shoppers sought to avoid her and I took my photo, unharried by the mob.

As we were so near, I took the opportunity to show Mrs T the original manuscript of A Tour Into Lincolnshire 1791, which is kept in Lincoln Library's strongroom.

Byng was born on the 18th of February 1743 and was educated at Westminster. After serving as a page to George II, he spent more than 20 years in the Army — as a Cornet in the Royal Horse Guards, a Captain in the 58th Foot, then rising to Lieutenant-Colonel in the 1st Foot Guards (today's Grenadiers) before finally retiring from military life in 1780. He probably went immediately to take up his monotonous duties in the Inland Revenue.

His early days were spent in Camps
His latter days were pass'd at Stamps

was his own brief summary of his life.

He had married Bridget Forrest in 1767 and she bore him 13 children. It was a fairly open secret in Byng's circle that his wife conducted a long affair with politician and diarist William Windham (curiously, Windham later married Bridget's sister Cecilia) and, to escape his tedious London life, Byng made more than a dozen tours. He wrote his diaries on the move before returning home to Duke Street, Piccadilly, to transcribe them in pen and ink and add his watercolours, poems, maps and copies of every bill from the inns where he stayed. But his works lay undiscovered until 1932 when a handful of manuscripts turned up at a second-hand bookseller's. The enterprising C. Bruyn Andrews set about gathering them together in four illustrated volumes between 1934 and 1938 as *The Torrington Diaries* — Byng inheriting the title of Viscount Torrington for the last 25 days of his life. The advent of war made it impossible to keep the volumes in print and, in 1954, Andrews' daughter Fanny produced a single-volume abridged edition which included the Lincolnshire tour. Most of the manuscripts were afterwards gifted to the local libraries in the counties where the rides took place.

A more up-to-date version, *Rides Round Britain*, was published by the Folio Society in 1996. It included the previously undiscovered Tour Into Kent of 1790 but, for reasons of "space", the Tour Into Lincolnshire was excluded.

Though written in an old-fashioned style of language, the Lincoln manuscript is surprisingly easy to read, humorous and without pretension. The small watercolours are charming and the hand-written bills presented at every inn record a startlingly different way of life.

The Rein Deer was not our first disappointment of the day. We had started out in Sleaford in search of the Angel Inn, where Byng spent 26th and 27th June 1791 waiting in vain for Colonel Bertie. A mountain of letters awaited him and he was fascinated by the town's market, which unfolded in front of his room. He enjoyed his food and thought his charge (7s 4d a night or about £30 today) reasonable. But he was scathing about the locals — *'there are few sightly men or handsome women to be seen in the country for the army gets one and Bond Street the other'* — and found Sleaford *'truly melancholy'*.

School was just breaking up as we began our search and, in all honesty, the young folk of Sleaford were as healthy and as good-looking as any we saw on our travels. Perhaps the Army and the bright lights of London are not such a draw two centuries on.

The Angel's owner was appointed Marquis of Bristol in 1826 and he celebrated by changing the name of the inn to the Bristol Arms. It boasted 16 chambers and six garrets and was Sleaford's largest and most select inn. But, possibly because of its size and the cost of maintaining the building, it closed in 1961 and is now a rather nondescript shopping arcade. The façade is hardly changed and you can walk under the archway where coaches squeezed through to the stable buildings at the rear.

A most helpful lady at the town's Tourist Information Centre had set us on the right road to finding the site of the old inn. So we asked about our next port of call, a 60-foot 'inland lighthouse' on the heath between Sleaford and Lincoln.

"Dunston Pillock?" she mouthed disbelievingly.

"Pillar. P-I-L-L-A-R," I quickly corrected.

"Never heard of it!"

The pillar had apparently been built to a height of 92 feet in 1751 by Sir Francis Dashwood, founder of the infamous Hell Fire Club, some say as a bet; others as a lighthouse to guide travellers across the lonely heathland.

In the winter of 1808, the 15-foot lantern was removed and replaced by a statue of King George III. A certain John Wilson fell to his death, aged 56, while putting the new addition in place. His tombstone at Harmston church is inscribed: "He who erected the noble King is here now laid by Death's sharp sting".

The king was also unceremoniously toppled and 30 feet chopped off the tower's height in 1941 when the structure was declared a danger to low-flying war planes.

Byng called it 'a waste of stone', so it would be gratifying to offer an unbiased modern opinion. But, try as we might, we could not find the infamous folly. We drove past Dunston in both directions, through Dunston village, even asked a villager who assured us we couldn't miss it. But miss it we did.

Dunston Pillock, indeed.

If you leave a door open in Lincolnshire, you may well be asked: "Do you come from Bardney?" The saying stems from the night monks refused to allow the bones of King Oswald into Bardney Abbey. During the night, a pillar of light shone skywards, convincing them Oswald was a saint. They left the abbey gates wide open from that day on.

Byng chose the Bardney road because he had read of many old religious houses in the area. In fact, in the 12th century, nine monasteries were founded in the Witham valley. As well as the high ecclesiastical status of Lincoln, the monks' major income was from wool, so a river with links to a trading port like Boston was vital.

As he left Lincoln, Byng saw carts hauling away the stones of Barlings Abbey. These were plundered to build local farms and houses, though the last remaining wall defied a team of horses and ropes in the 19th century and is still visible today, together with earthworks and ponds that clearly show the layout of the old monastery. In 1537, the abbot and four of his canons were hanged on the orders of Henry VIII for rebelling against the Dissolution as part of the famous Lincolnshire Rising.

To cross the River Witham, Byng took a short ferry which has given its name to the village where now stands a bridge and the Tyrwhitt Arms. From Short Ferry, he rode on to see what remained of Stainfield Hall, the deserted seat of the Tyrwhitts, one of Lincolnshire's oldest families whose name, like others in the county, derives from the lapwing or trewitt. He found much of it pulled down with just some *'tolerable apartments and some bad family pictures'*. A solitary stone gate pier is all that survives today.

Byng continued to Tupholme Abbey, *'whereof some small remains are attach'd to a farm house'*. Fortunately, thanks to the Heritage Trust of Lincolnshire and the Friends of Tupholme Abbey, the site was bought in 1988 and there are now interpretation panels, a picnic place and a flock of Soay sheep. The site is proving a haven for wildlife in an otherwise intensely farmed landscape.

At Kirkstead, he painted a watercolour of the last remaining corner of Kirkstead Abbey. Remarkably, the same fragment still stands, surrounded by cows and farmland. The nearby Old Hall, built from the abbey's stones, was being renovated with an Historic Building Grant from the district and county councils as we drove past.

Byng told a passing farmer: *'Your neighbourhood seem'd to be famed formerly for religion: now I suppose a curate can take charge of ye all!'* before making tracks for lunch. *'At one o'clock, tired and hungry, I stopp'd before the Angel, a poor ale house, in the mean village of Bradney, and enquired of the landlord: Have you any corn for horses or meat for man?'*

The Angel is now Bards Family Pub & Restaurant and manages to thrive in a village badly hit by the closure in 2001 of the sugar beet factory which was the area's biggest employer.

No sign of a landlord here. Just a pleasant, if harassed-looking lady who served us the dish of the day, delicious fresh cod goujons with chips.

Birthday cards adorned the windows of the modern bar but there seemed a certain tension in the air. "This might explain it," ventured Mrs T, pointing to a pile of menu cards. Printed on them was a warm welcome from the landlord and landlady. Except his name had been scribbled out of each one in ballpoint pen.

At the Lea Gate Inn we were welcomed by a strangely-coloured wire-haired terrier — totally white at the front; all black at the rear. We soon discovered the cause of these unusual markings when he began to rub his back end against the underside of the car near to the still-scorching and sooty exhaust pipe.

This night stop had severely tested our powers of research. Byng referred only to the Tumby Swan in his diary. A tour of both Tumby and neighbouring Tumby Woodside having proved fruitless, we consulted Byng's original bill. Alongside engravings of a swan and a lion, it gives the landlord's name "Thos Hall, Tumby" and underneath adds "from Leeds Gates" — the breakthrough we needed.

Further enquiry revealed that the Leeds Gate toll marked the start of the Lincolnshire Fens. Travellers risking the treacherous crossing of boggy marshland on dark winter nights were guided by a flaming beacon attached to the side of the toll-keeper's house. The ring which held that beacon is still in position today, on the side of the Lea Gate Inn, though there's no longer a toll and they give their address as Coningsby. Built in 1542, the inn wall also boasts a sign which reads: "This gate hangs high and hinders none; Victual yours'en and pass along".

Outside stood a gallows where executed criminals were left to hang as a warning to others.

Nowadays the inn, no longer thatched, is one of contrasts

and, one suspects, may have lost some of its olde worlde charm during extensions and refurbishment which added eight bedrooms around the turn of the new millennium.

Byng's *double-bedded room was like that of a farm house with a deal door and a latch and joices white wash'd'.* Ours — the Griffiths Room — was spacious and light but had been furnished from a repro catalogue and showed the signs of a recent serious damp problem.

The bar area boasts a low ceiling and a huge inglenook fireplace that hides a priest hole. The restaurant, converted from old stables, is less appealing, its lack of atmosphere not helped by a karaoke piano belting out *The Best of Elton John* to no one in particular as the keys pumped eerily without human assistance. What is so abhorrent about conversation? The elderly diners on the next table had not seen each other for several years and had much gossip to exchange. They showed no sign of bursting into a chorus of *Crocodile Rock* at any time during their meal.

The helpful and chatty barman was Portuguese — "my friends still won't believe the sea is brown in England!" — and several of the customers Norwegian. Very cosmopolitan, but not quite the slice of Old England we were expecting. The inn is listed in several major guides, so perhaps things improve when the local crowd gathers and Mine Hosts are in attendance.

5ᴛʜ Jᴜʟʏ 1791 *In our parlour, hung a picture of the King of Prussia so like Admiral Byng, with the same round, smooth, unmeaning face. Our charge was extraordinary cheap for we had for dinner (4s 3d) a neck of mutton boil'd with caper sauce and vegetables, a roasted duck, tart, collard eel and a bottle of port wine and ale.*
I know several men who indulged in liquor and yet preserv'd their looks and health by resolving upon exercise.

Room 101

Tattershall — Donington — Spalding — Holbeach

Byng headed off early from Tumby to breakfast at the Angel Inn at Tattershall and to view the castle. In order to hit the relevant opening times, we were able to make a gentler start to the day. Having breakfasted well at the Lea Gate, we contented ourselves with coffee at the Fortescue Arms in the market place. The Angel changed its name in the 1840s and is still thriving. The Fortesques were lords of the manor who had famously incurred the wrath of villagers in 1754 by selling stained glass from the parish church windows for £50 and replacing some of them with clear glass, leaving the rest open to the elements for the next 50 years.

Lord Curzon of Kedleston tried and failed to find the missing glass at the beginning of the 20th century. Much more successful was his intervention to save Tattershall Castle, one of the major landmarks of Lincolnshire and described by Byng as *'the grandest piece of brickwork in the kingdom'.* Built in 1455 by Ralph, Lord Cromwell, the Lord High Treasurer of England, as much for display as for protection, the castle had fallen into wrack and ruin by the time Byng noted its three *'antique stone chimney pieces laden with armorial bearings, which should be taken care off and might be removed'.*

By 1911, when all the floors had collapsed, the fireplaces had indeed been removed and were destined for the

American antiques market. When Lord Curzon, a childhood visitor to Tattershall, heard of this, he immediately bought the property, tracked down the departing stonework and set about returning the castle to its former glories. He then presented it to the National Trust, which opens it regularly to visitors. On the day we arrived, the sun shone on the magnificent brickwork of the castle walls and, at the top of a ruined outbuilding, peahens tended their brood of young as strutting peacocks called out a warning to anyone silly enough to go too near. Atmosphere and history ooze from the rooms of the tower and the battlements give an unrivalled view of this part of Lincolnshire, over the River Witham as far as Boston. It was difficult to leave such a magnificent setting, but lunch called and, like Byng, we headed south.

At the end of my third year at Wintringham Grammar School in Grimsby, the chemistry master was handing back the class's exercise books for the final time. He remarked on how well everyone had done and wished us all the best for the summer holidays. "Just one thing before you go," he said as we ached for the bell to sound. "Which one of you is Taylor?" I slowly raised my hand, face reddening and heart pumping as all eyes swivelled in my direction. He stared at me as if I had been beamed into his laboratory from the Starship Enterprise or had changed my name halfway through the term and forgotten to tell him. I had been in his class for a whole year; he had marked my work on a weekly basis but I had made so little impression on him he couldn't even put a face to the name. Imagine what that does to a 14-year-old's self-confidence.

Donington's a bit like that. After 20 years of living in Lincolnshire, a quarter of those working on various local newspapers in the county, I could not call to mind ever having been to Donington or even having seen a picture of it.

I had never met anyone who came from Donington, had not passed through it on the way to somewhere more memorable. In all honesty, I had never heard of it.

Yet there it was on the map, 11 miles south-west of Boston on the A52, the birthplace of Captain Matthew Flinders who charted and named much of Australia and was then himself forgotten when the warring French stole his journals and claimed his discoveries for themselves.

Byng called the town Dunnington, though it was also known as Donnington (already scarred by an identity crisis), when he called at the Red Cow for lunch on his way to meet up at long last with Colonel Bertie at Spalding. *'A small market town where I dined comfortably on a shoulder of lamb, peas and tart in a quiet house'* was all he could think to write about his sojourn in 1791. Yet the Universal British Directory for that year notes that: "Donnington, or Dunnington, is very much improved within the last ten years, is noted for a large sale of hemp and hemp-seed and has a port for barges by which goods are carried to and from Boston and the Washes".

Quietly pondering whatever happened to Donington's extra 'n', we drove slowly into the town, keeping our eyes peeled for our next stop. A sign to our left announced THE RED   OW CAR PARK. "This missing consonant problem is turning into an epidemic," mused Mrs T as we bumped our way over a pot-holed entrance and past a pensioners' Pop-In centre before parking the Z3.

"It must be this way," I pointed as we followed an over-grown alleyway into the courtyard of what must once have been a thriving inn. But, sadly, no more. The sight that greeted us was a boarded-up eyesore with glass, wood and old metal kegs strewn around. We made our way to the front of the building, where a council enforcement notice was pinned to the chained-up front door, ordering the owners to make safe the entrances to prevent further vandalism.

The post office opposite was closed for lunch but enquiries of a nearby estate agent revealed the Red Cow had closed some two months before.

"Will it reopen?"

"Ooh, I don't know about that," said the agent.

"Will they knock it down?"

"They can't — it's listed."

With digestive juices running on maximum, we looked around for somewhere else to have lunch. The Peacock and the Black Bull were both around in Byng's time; the kebab takeaway was not. But depression had set in. Donington's somewhat melancholy air had got through to us and we vowed to move on.

"We could cheat and call at the Bell at Pinchbeck," said my co-traveller as we headed out through Quadring and Gosberton and the mood lightened. "Byng stopped there on a previous tour to shelter from the rain."

"It's a thin connection, but okay," I agreed reluctantly. "If it's still there and it looks nice."

It was still there and looked clean and well-managed. Better still, there was a small restaurant next door offering fresh Grimsby haddock as its speciality.

But this was Monday. And the Bell had decided there was not enough money to be made this early in the week and had kept its doors firmly shut. Ditto the restaurant.

Time was when pubs had to open at hours specified by the government. Close for just one session and risk losing your licence. My grandfather would have loved the freedom offered by the new licensing laws. His customers at the Saracen's Head on Grimsby Dock were mostly trawlermen. At lunchtime, they crowded into the pub's huge bar, spent well and generally behaved themselves. At night, the staff often outnumbered the clientele and those lost souls who did find their way in were often drunk and looking for trouble. Lights burned for no-one's benefit and the barmaids chatted amongst themselves while counting the hours until they could go home again. Not that life was ever dull for long with Grandad, whose broad build I inherited but none of his fearlessness.

After leaving home at 14 when his father remarried, Tommy Taylor sought a life in the licensed trade, sleeping under the bar counter and taking boxing lessons so he might be more use to his landlady boss. Finishing school in the First World War trenches of the Somme, where he was gassed, bayoneted and shot at, just added to his air of indestructibility. When he felt one of his customers had overstepped the mark or gone beyond his drinking limit, Grandad's thumb would point towards the door. "Out" was all he ever said on these occasions but a hush would descend over the smoke room as the regulars prayed the miscreant would not make the same mistake as others before him and ask: "Can you put me out?"

Our stomachs were now rumbling so loud as to drown out the car radio. But there was to be no joy at our next scheduled stop, either. I had managed to obtain a 2001 artist's impression of a rejuvenated White Hart in Spalding market place. It showed a small group of well-dressed business people perusing a menu under the hotel's restored canopy, torn between the spacious Main Bar and Coach House restaurant or the more intimate Welland Bar down a side passage. What greeted us were men in hard hats and boots, busily looking at plans while scratching their heads. Digger drivers carried materials to and fro within the fenced-off building site.

Byng spent two nights at the White Hart in 1791. Mary

Queen of Scots beat him to it in 1566, though the inn served its first customer as far back as 1377. The Taylors in 2003 were not even to be granted a drink and a snack. According to the agent's particulars: "The new-look White Hart, when completed, will boast 9,600 square feet of pub and restaurant development with six staff parking spaces, available as one or two units. The developers are working closely with English Heritage and South Holland District Council to ensure that the completed development provides a compromise between building conservation and practicality. The front part of the inn has been retained, with the less attractive outbuildings behind being demolished."

That would surely have met with the approval of the Spalding Gentleman's Society, founded in 1712 so its members could discuss "antiquities and read the *Tatler*, a newly published London periodical". Members over the years have included Sir Isaac Newton and Alfred Lord Tennyson and there is still a private museum of historic relics in Broad Street.

What the esteemed gentlemen might not have found so pleasing today was the incessant traffic around Sheep Market and the difficulty in finding a parking place. "Forgotten Lincolnshire" has suddenly sprung into the minds of a new generation of maniac drivers though, in fairness, dangerous oldies are as much a problem as rampaging youngsters.

Spalding is the centre of the flower industry; more daffodils are grown here than anywhere in Britain; the River Welland runs through the centre and there are elegant Georgian buildings in the conservation area. But on this weekday afternoon in June, "peaceful market town" was taking the publicity spin a little too far.

By the time we arrived at the newly-painted Chequers at Holbeach, we could have eaten anything. Well, not quite anything. The restaurant offers "a varied selection of dishes for all ages and tastes". We probably had too much of both to appreciate "rod of onion rings — a six inch erection or a full 12 inches". And "ten pieces of scampi" seemed far too precise to be worth the risk.

But we settled happily for vegetable cannelloni from the specials menu, together with cheesy garlic bread and a choice of new potatoes, jacket spud or chips (why *do* the English serve potatoes with pasta?). With a very acceptable Merlot red wine and some water, the bill came to £26.95 for two. Like Byng's before us, our '*charge was extraordinary cheap*'.

Barneys Restaurant is well designed on a modern jazz theme and there are dozens of dishes available, not all dependent on the ubiquitous deep-fat fryer. Twisters Bar, at the front of the hotel overlooking the High Street, is open all day and was proving popular with contractors from a nearby power station site when we arrived.

In Roman times, the sea reached as far as High Street. Holbeach's first inhabitants were probably slaves and outlaws brave enough to suffer the harsh conditions of a no-man's land between the ancient kingdoms of Mercia and East Anglia. By the early 19th century, it was two miles inland and, thanks to yet more land reclamation, Holbeach is now seven miles from the coast. It became important as a coaching town, offering shelter to travellers heading for Long Sutton and the dangerous journey across the marshes to Norfolk.

Holbeach went into decline in the 20th century but in the past three or four years has begun to fight back and attract shops like Tesco. Househunters leaving the congested south of England for a quieter rural existence have filled many of the empty properties. It is to be hoped that the influx of new blood will save Holbeach from that evil that so afflicts cut-off communities on long winter nights — an overwhelming desire to play country and western music. There's even a shop in town devoted to the craze.

A blue plaque in High Street marks the birthplace of Sir Norman Angell, one-time vine planter, ditch digger, prospector and reporter for the *San Francisco Chronicle*. In 1933 he won the Nobel Peace Prize for his book *The Great Illusion*, which set out to establish the fallacy of the idea that conquest and war brought a nation great economic advantage, access to trade and raw materials. As radio bulletins blasted out more bad news from Iraq, Israel and Afghanistan, we mused it was time for a reprint to be made available to the White House library.

Byng had his own poignant reminder of war and troubled family times when he spotted in a portrait of Frederick William I of Prussia a striking resemblance to the uncle whose name he shared.

For his failure to relieve Minorca, blockaded by a French fleet, and for retreating to Gibraltar, Admiral John Byng was contentiously found guilty of neglect of duty and shot in 1757 at Portsmouth, in the words of Voltaire *"pour encourager les autres"*.

Back at the hotel, it was time for us to settle down for the night. "Your room's the first one on the first floor," explained a helpful barman. For £49 a night we were treated to an amazing array of furniture, mostly too big for the room, a decor of chocolate and banana yellow and a white tiled bathroom reminiscent of an asylum. With every step, the giant wardrobe creaked and banged and the bed headboard tapped out its harmony against the back wall. No monkey business tonight. And not much sleep, either, as the room looked directly on to a glass-strewn, corrugated iron roof and a beer cooler that kept up a constant hum until morning.

A pity the care taken in refurbishing the rest of the hotel had not extended to our quarters. As we checked out next morning, Mrs T pointed to the number that was written at the top of our bill: we had been consigned to Room 101.

The White Hart, Spilsby

6ᴛʜ Jᴜʟʏ 1791 *A long delay to our dinner when sad cookery spoil'd everything; the mutton of this country is shockingly large and coarse. I eat nothing but beans or young potatoes, which can scarcely be spoiled. To them I order'd slices of bacon broil'd, which the Coll said was a rash action; rather say, Col, that is a rasher action! After dinner we eagerly walk'd to survey what might remain of the old family seat of the Berties at Eresby, near this town, which seat was burn'd down about 30 years ago.*

Bill for 2 nights: £1 4s 11d *This morning I was awaken'd by the barkings and fightings of dogs upon the market place. Such nuisance and noise is intolerable; one dog can disturb a whole town. Oh for a dog tax!*

The Fosdyke saga

Boston — Spilsby

John Byng was not a happy man; practical, enthusiastic, sentimental even, but not happy. He had much to be miserable about. His brother had inherited the title of Viscount Torrington and with it the family's wealth and power. His wife was a well-known adulteress who took advantage of his long tours to meet openly with her lover. He hated London life and his boring job.

So moments of pure joy are rare and sought after by his biographers in a bid to prove Byng was a well-rounded character. One such incident occurred in 1790 on his Tour In The Midlands when he happened across his own little piece of paradise. *'I came in 5 miles to the banks of the washes where is a public house — call'd Fosdike — of the bathing sort, where is a large room for company, some good bed chambers and a bathing house. If a person would study to find out a quiet place with a fine sand in front and good roads with a pleasant country behind, and with cheap living, then this is the spot. I had the house to myself and drank tea most comfortably in the great room, with a view over the sand, beautiful when the tide is in.'*

His mood had darkened by the following year when he revisited as part of his Tour Into Lincolnshire: *'At Fossdyke House, a mean bathing place where I drank tea last year, we stopp'd for an hour. It is a melancholy place, for we saw only one girl who waited on us, but our intention serv'd well for variety.'*

As we finished off our vegetarian breakfast at the Chequers Hotel in Holbeach — a huge plateful of scrambled egg, beans, tomatoes, mushrooms and toast — Mrs T was smiling to herself and I gave her a quizzical gaze.

"A penny for them?"

"I'm really looking forward to Fosdyke. It sounds beautiful."

What can a man do in the face of such eagerness and optimism? I tried to let her down gently: "It's not like it was in Byng's day, you know. That was 213 years ago and even he had gone off the place by the next time he visited..."

The smile persisted.

"...and the pub's not there any more. Boston Library can't find any reference to it at all..." (I decided not to mention that what they had found was a newspaper cutting from the 1970s, labelling Fosdyke the 'Village of the Cursed' following a spate of suicides and the loss at sea of the crew of a local seal boat.)

The smile changed to a satisfied grin.

"...and it's very flat round here. You didn't like Cambridge because the damp got to your chest, remember."

But it was all to no avail. In her mind's eye, Fosdyke had become a cross between a sandy Cornwall cove and Treasure Island. Only a matter of time before she asked for the names of local estate agents.

So it was with trepidation that some time later I pulled the car off the racetrack that is the A17 at the side of a lonely bridge spanning a muddy drain. Heavy lorries pounded the metal struts in both directions as a solitary building looked forlornly down over a gravelled car park.

"Why are we stopping?" asked Mrs T, surprised. "Is there a problem?"

"No, we're here. Paradise."

A council information board under the bridge explained how the course of the drain had been altered over the years to accommodate barges; how the sands disappeared as it silted up and how the original bridge had been replaced, first by a toll crossing and then the current ironwork.

In Byng's day, a guide was hired for threepence a horse to escort travellers to the opposite bank *'inventing or magnifying the danger you might have sustained without his pilotage'.*

The Fosdyke Inn still stands but it's a private house now, and not so near the water as it used to be. The Ship Inn, a roadside oasis, has taken its place. But it was still early and there were no signs of life, there or anywhere else in the vicinity. Just the deafening, speeding lorries that sucked you into their slipstream if you were foolish enough to get too close to the road.

"What does Foss Dyke mean?" asked a disappointed voice as we climbed back into the BMW.

"Loosely translated, something like Shit Creek."

"And no sign of a paddle. Shall we go?"

Boston surprised us with its charm and grandeur. There are lots of old buildings surrounding its vibrant market place and shopping streets. Sadly, the Peacock Inn is not one of them. Built between 1750 and 1780, the Peacock was a large coaching inn. In 1880, Queen Victoria's son Alfred, the Duke of Edinburgh, stayed there and it was renamed the Peacock and Royal. It closed in 1965 and the building was demolished. A rather featureless Sixties brick construction replaced it and now houses Boston's branch of Boots.

The town has a history of shooting itself in the foot. It was one of England's first mediæval ports and boomed in the 1760s, when the vast Holland Fen was drained to grow crops which were then shipped far and wide. But the seeds of decline had been planted in 1608, when well-wishers stood on the dockside to wave farewell to the departing Pilgrim Fathers. The religious dissenters set sail for Holland, then America, establishing their own Boston in Massachusetts. America became the great trading nation and there was a need for ports on the west coast of England. Farewell Boston's heyday! More recent foolhardiness has come in the shape of John Adams Way — a 'ring' road which, instead of skirting Boston, ploughs a destructive furrow right through the heart of the old town.

Byng traversed only cobble stones to arrive at the Peacock on 5th July 1791. He was not impressed: *'The evening was so cold as to force us to sit over a fire at coming in, when we might have wished for some tolerable fish at supper but the cod fish stunk so as not to be endured. So, likewise in the inn of a famous wine merchant (Mr Fydell), the wine was not drinkable. One might have expected something less than poison. Brandy and water, and peevishness, soon hurried us to bed.'*

Thomas Fydell was MP for Boston and three times Mayor. He lived at the magnificent Fydell House "undoubtedly the grandest house in Boston", which was built in the early 1700s and still stands today beside the mediæval Guildhall in a part of town which is undergoing much restoration and improvement.

The market place is cobbled once more for the benefit of pedestrians, but traffic is still allowed through and approaches unexpectedly from all directions — a sure-fire recipe for disaster.

If John Byng were to ride into Spilsby today, he would have little trouble finding his way around. A quiet, 18th-century market town, it remains largely untouched by the excesses of modern-day living. Byng accompanied Colonel

Bertie to what remained of Eresby House, which had burned down in 1769. All they found were the twin pillars of the approach. Just one remains today, topped by a magnificent urn. They had more luck at the parish church where monuments to the Willoughby and Bertie families are the main attraction.

Apart from the addition of a bay window in Victorian times, the White Hart Hotel has stood unaltered in the market place since 1660. It escaped the fire which destroyed more than 100 mostly thatched houses in 1706 and led to the rebuilding of Spilsby in the Georgian style. It is still a popular meeting place on Monday market days, with a bar, lounge and function rooms plus cosy log fires in the winter.

We were tired and a little downhearted when we arrived but the friendly staff soon lifted our spirits as we took our place in the lounge bar to peruse a menu of freshly-prepared food. I ordered prawn korma with rice, chutney, papadom and chapatti for Mrs T and Grimsby haddock in batter with chips for myself.

We barely had time to finish our first drink before the biggest plate of curry I have ever seen arrived in front of me. "Mine's the haddock," I explained. "Oh, sorry," said the barmaid. "Because you asked for the korma first, I thought it was for you. I did you extra." An interesting insight into Lincolnshire etiquette.

The White Hart is obviously still at the hub of the community. A party of sports-jacketed Rotarians had time for a preprandial drink before making their way through to the restaurant. A coachload of youngsters with learning difficulties replaced them at the bar. And the sound of a traditional Lincolnshire greeting could be heard from the neighbouring room: "Nah then y'owd basta'd, ah thawt you were deäd." Well, this is Tennyson country!

Our cosy double room in yellow and blue with pine

furniture was spotlessly clean and the bathroom boasted fluffy towels and a bathrobe.

A party of anglers leaving early for a day at the side of the Lincolnshire drains disturbed our sleep so we had a lie-in before taking our time over a breakfast of beans and scrambled eggs on toast, mushrooms and tomatoes that would have fed at least three. Our bill of £77.40 was the best value for money of our whole tour and we were a little sorry to be setting out once again into the unknown, under the watchful eye of Spilsby's most famous son.

A statue of the explorer Sir John Franklin, born in 1796, dominates the market place. After an illustrious naval career, Franklin supposedly discovered the Northwest Passage through the frozen Arctic. Though he left in 1845 with two ships and 134 men, he never returned and he and his men perished in the ice. Still, a bit of bad news was never enough to prevent the Victorians erecting a statue to "a great British explorer".

I prefer the attitude of another Lincolnshire worthy, Sir Joseph Banks, the botanist who sailed around the world on the Endeavour with Captain Cook and was President of the Royal Society for 42 years. He insisted that no statues or memorials be erected upon his death. A Knight Commander and Director of Kew Gardens, Banks did not escape the wrath of John Byng, who rode out from Spilsby to see the family seat at Revesby. *The park is flat, dismal and unimproved; the house mean and uncomfortable. But when a man sets himself up for a wild, eccentric character and can reside in a corner house in Soho-Square; of course his country seat will be a filthy neglected spot.'*

After Banks's death, his nephew James Banks Stanhope built an enormous new house in 1843 but it fell into dereliction and the magnificent iron gates present a gloomy prospect to modern-day passers-by.

Fortunately, Sir Joseph was not at home when Byng and Colonel Bertie called. The housekeeper showed them round and they left their cards and travelled on to neighbouring Scrivelsby Hall, 'where Mr Repton is here employ'd to improve the grounds'.

Byng was an acquaintance of Humphry Repton, who invented the term "landscape gardening" to express his theory that the art requires "the united powers of the landscape painter and the practical gardener". Byng preferred the more natural surroundings of rivers and parkland and found Repton a man of 'so many words that he is not easily shaken off; he asserts so much and assumes so much as to make me irritable, for he is one who is never wrong; and therefore why debate with him?'.

Happily, in the name of keeping the peace, Repton was not around this time, nor the master of Scrivelsby. The maid servant showed them around the house, or what was left of it after a bad fire 30 years before, but she proved 'stupid to an extreme and ill merited our two shillings'.

Our own route to Scrivelsby began as a narrow road which became a track and then, worryingly, a gated path across a field of sheep. Though the burned-out ruins were replaced by a new house at the beginning of the 19th century, this too was pulled down after the Second War by Colonel John Dymoke, who converted the Tudor gatehouse into his home.

The magnificent crowned stone lion which sits on top of the entrance gate gives the only clue that the Dymoke family have held the title of King's and Queen's Champion since the reign of Richard I. Originally it was the champion's duty to ride on a white charger, dressed in full armour, into Westminster Hall during the coronation ceremony to throw down his gauntlet and challenge any person who dared to deny the sovereign's right to the throne.

It is not recorded whether Colonel Dymoke, at the coronation of the present Queen, was disappointed to be asked instead merely to carry the Royal Standard. *'How strange it seems,'* mused Byng, *'that officers requiring superior courage or politeness should be hereditary honors; and that a champion might prove a coward, and a master of the ceremonies a driver of stage-coaches.'*

Colonel Bertie's incessant search for family relics took the travellers to Welton and Willoughby, where they encountered a heavy storm and Byng advised a stop at the Six Bells ale house. He was overruled and they headed instead for Willoughby church *'much out of repair'*. Byng was not in the best of moods and no mention is made of Willoughby's most famous son, Captain John Smith. Smith's father, George, was a tenant farmer of Sir Peregrine Bertie, the "brave Lord Willoughby" who had commanded Elizabeth I's English troops fighting the Spanish in Holland.

Not content with a farmer's life, the young John learnt to fight and set off to battle the Turks. He won the rank of Captain before being captured and sold as a slave in Constantinople. He escaped back to London and set sail for America in 1606 but argued with so many of his fellow adventurers that he was under arrest when the party landed to found what was later to become Virginia.

It was not until his second summer there that he was elected state president. He used his leadership skills to trade with the Indians and made a lasting friendship with the princess Pocahontas. His practical knowledge was put to use in erecting buildings in the 'mud and stud' style of his native Lincolnshire — a mix of earth, straw and water on rough timber which survives today in buildings such as the Royal Oak at Mareham-le-Fen.

The welcoming church of St Helena in Willoughby now

boasts windows depicting the life of the remarkable Captain Smith, as well as the coat of arms of Peregrine Bertie, whose tomb is in St James's, Spilsby.

We were left to reflect that Lincolnshire has its fair share of men who have achieved fame and influenced world events... and that John Byng could not summon up a good word to say about any of them!

7ᴛʜ Jᴜʟy 1791 *Our ride was now over the sands to Skegness Inn, a vile, shabby bathing place... the Coll, with difficulty, prevail'd upon the old hostess (une diablesse) to allow us to enter a mean parlour below and to have some food therein. A walk upon the sea-sand, and to sniff up the wholesome breeze, till we thought we might return to our landlady's bar room where we had some miserable smelts and some raw, rank cold beef put before us. There is no garden, no walk, no billiard room nor anything for comfort or temptation. If a good house were built here with a clever landlord, it would draw much company and answer well. If we had intended a night stop here, we had been undone for every bed was engaged and no abode nearer than Spillsby: for no ale house at Burgh was fit for a bag man.*

No room at the inn

Horncastle — Skegness

I've never really taken to Horncastle, despite its history — the Romans founded a settlement here and called it Banovallum — and its quaintness. There's a market and a local newspaper, the *Horncastle News*, of the sort I should really appreciate, with reports of church fêtes and village football battling for space with sightings of the legendary Wolds panther. It was also voted the Antiques Town of Britain 2001. Maybe that's why I took against it. Spending a day in Horncastle is like being marooned in a gigantic flea market where shop after shop displays heap upon heap of discarded clutter, or "kelter" as they say in Lincolnshire.

For certain members of my family, that makes it a paradise. My brother-in-law (even his own family call him Del Boy) lives in a world of buying and selling, of lock-up garages, of bartering and bargain-hunting. So Horncastle is his nirvana. And my mother, the only woman I know who keeps a garage full of old spare white goods — "you never know when something might break down" — and tables, would happily retire to Horncastle and disappear into a roomful of old knick-knacks, last heard of shouting "they only want £2.50 for the whole boxful".

The pubs aren't bad, either. But they're not great. They're just... okay.

At one time, I could have said Horncastle had done

47

nothing to offend me. But that changed in 1999 when I let my heart rule my head and chose a dentist in the town based solely on his glossy full-page advertisement in a county magazine. His surgery in the shadow of St Mary's church was beautifully decorated, a complete suit of armour in the tasteful waiting room, the very latest equipment upstairs in his surgery, a bevy of helpful assistants. For hour after hour he sweated away at reshaping my neglected mouth. And all the time he was being investigated by the British Dental Council for carrying out unnecessary work. Shortly after I paid my extortionate bill, he was struck off. So now every time I chew a piece of bread or clean my teeth, I have a reason to really hate Horncastle. But I don't. It just does nothing for me — like opera, like improvisational jazz, like algebra. I can see that there's something there but it's wasted on me.

Byng had a similar feeling: '*To Horncastle where we dined upon a good cold dinner when I ate more than usual having been half starved at Spilsby. And the wine being found tolerable, we finish'd our bottle and resolv'd to stay the night. Nothing to be seen in this town, only famous for its horse fair.*' And they don't hold that Whitsuntide extravaganza any more.

So it was with an air of new beginnings that we drove through the town and into the car park of the Bull Hotel — one of the few inns on the tour still with its original name. Byng had turned up unannounced — that was the way then. We had wanted to be sure of a room so had booked well in advance and sent a cheque for £25 some weeks before so that we should not be disappointed. And, as we pulled under the arch where once mail coaches discharged their weary passengers, we were pleasantly surprised. The hotel had obviously undergone considerable refurbishment and the newly-painted signs pointing the way to reception gleamed in the June evening sunlight.

A clever window arrangement allowed the barmaid to see us entering reception once she had finished pulling a pint in the busy bar. She turned to watch us enter with our suitcase and bags, then stared with a look of horror. It was several seconds before she said hesitantly: "Yes..?"

"The name's Taylor; we have a double en suite room booked for tonight."

"Here?"

"Yes."

"Tonight?"

This was in danger of turning into rehearsal night for an excruciatingly poor amateur theatre production.

"I'll get the boss."

We put down our bags and glanced around, double checking we had not wandered into a neighbouring house by mistake. No, this really was the Bull Hotel, Horncastle, just as it said on our itinerary.

Some ten minutes later, the landlord and landlady appeared.

"There's been a bit of a mix-up. Your room's not ready," an apologetic Mine Host informed us.

"That's okay. We can have a beer while we wait. When will it be ready?"

"August the first. The builders have let us down."

"That's two months away. But we sent a cheque."

"We've only just taken over," butted in Mine Hostess. "The only cheque we had was from a man — he was from Monaco, too, funnily enough — doing a car rally."

"The Tour of Lincolnshire, perhaps?"

She ignored this remark. "But I sent his cheque back."

All these people winging in from Monte-Carlo. What a pity they had no rooms. It was obviously becoming the new in-scene for the world's bright young things. Skiing in

Gstaad, yachting in Mustique, a pint of mild at the Bull in Horncastle.

They explained that, while we were waiting for them, they had been busy booking us into another hotel in the town, "Best Western, four poster and everything". When we explained that we were only interested in inns that had been visited by John Byng and that it was not worth us staying at a different hotel in Horncastle, they kindly rang the Vine in Skegness to see if they could accommodate us for the night. We refused the offer of a drink and packed our bags back into the boot of the car.

Sorry, Horncastle. You had your second chance and you blew it.

The incident had two postscripts. I was back in Lincolnshire in August and rang again, but there were still no rooms at the inn. "They're saying three to four weeks," explained a weary voice. And the cheque never arrived — though it wasn't cashed either. Let's hope the other man from Monaco got his.

Disappointed but not downhearted, we drove to Skegness, where tattooed youths and pasty-faced girls prowled the noisy streets in search of excitement and the seafront Embassy Theatre proclaimed the imminent arrival of rock and rollers Showaddywaddy. Our own three steps to heaven were via Seacroft and the golf links to the more genteel end of 'Skeggy', down a long drive to an ivy-clad building that would not have been out of place in the heart of the countryside.

The receptionist at the Vine Hotel couldn't have been nicer. We explained our predicament and she checked us in to a cosy double room. When we came down to the bar, she was the one who served us our welcoming pints of cold Guinness and prawn sandwiches with crisps. And she it was, too, who made sure the heated towel rail was switched off before our room turned into a sauna on one of the hottest nights of the year. There were other staff around but she took it upon herself to make sure we were comfortable and had everything we needed. It is amazing how one interested employee can make all the difference between a 'stay' and an 'experience'.

The Vine is everything you could ask for in a seaside hotel. Oak tables, log fires in winter, hand-pulled real ales from the local Batemans brewery. It's a locals' pub, too, with darts, dominoes, crib and quiz nights.

Starting out as a small farmhouse in the middle of the 17th century, by 1772 it had become The Skegness Inn, a key drop-off site for local smugglers. The skeleton of a customs man was found during refurbishments in 1900.

Alfred Lord Tennyson composed poetry in the grounds. The bar still bears his name, though the tree where he carved his initials succumbed to Dutch elm disease, despite expensive attempts to rescue it.

The next morning we breakfasted well and paid our bill of £88 for the room. Byng's advice was taken to heart. For a good house has been built which does draw much company. The Vine is popular with the blue-rinse set as well as with holidaymakers and golfers. There is a huge function room for weddings and conferences, a bowling green and a beautiful garden where we sat and watched a robin feed her enormous baby only inches from our table.

At my porch the swallow may build,
The white-owl in my barn shall grow fat;
The robin a shelter I'll yield,
And the crumbs he shall pick from the mat. JB

12th July 1791 To Barton where we expected a goodish inn but the best appear'd dismal and casemented! However, we must sleep. Tea drank and orders given for supper, we walked thro' the town, which is mean and dirty, and to the river side where the passage boats lye. Here is an inn where we might have fared better than at The George. We shut ourselves up, eat our mutton chops and of a great coarse Holybut. Then quickly to our rooms...

Bill for 1 night: 9s 11d Most glad to part from Barton which is a nasty, gloomy place.

DAY SIX

Don't go there!

*Louth — Saltfleet — Cleethorpes —
Great Limber — Barton-on-Humber*

'**W**hy are you going to Barton?" my niece enquired
with a pained expression. "Do you have to go?"
"Sort of," I explained. "It's for research. I'm
staying at The George."

Her face fell. "You'll probably be all right. You're not
going at the weekend, are you?"

"Friday, in the BMW."

"Oh dear."

"Why are you going to Barton?" asked my brother-in-
law. "My friend Pete says you go to Scunthorpe for a girl and
a good time and to Barton for a fight."

My journalist pal looked concerned: "Barton? You're not
taking Victoria with you, are you?"

The rates for car hire at Humberside International
Airport are reasonable and the staff at Europcar quite
friendly. They couldn't get the computer to work and they
didn't know what to do with an upgrade voucher. Oh, and it's
not so international that they're open on Sundays. But the
Fiat Stilo they had waiting was suitably anonymous in
battleship grey with several scratches (all marked on an
accompanying plan). Just the thing for a night in Barton.

The sports car stowed away in a friend's drive, the
evening passed with an air of tension. The George had
asked us to confirm our booking of an en suite double with
breakfast. "Perhaps they've forgotten and won't have room,"

53

said Mrs T as she dialled them on the mobile. "Yes, they're looking forward to seeing us," she sighed resignedly as she clipped the phone back into place. "Wish it was mutual."

The morning had begun much more brightly as we left Skegness to cross the Wolds and head for Louth. We had hardly left 'Skeggy' before we took the first of several diversions. Gunby Hall, the seat of the Massingberd family since it was built by the 2nd Baronet in 1700, has been described as a giant doll's house, its three storeys gazing down on lawns, yew hedges and cedar trees. It was given to the National Trust by a grateful Field Marshal Sir Archibald Montgomery Massingberd, who had appealed to the King to prevent demolition of the hall for a runway in the Second World War. The gardens are magnificent but we found the house a little creepy and were pleased to note that Byng had felt the same: *'a most melancholy place; suicide in every room'*.

As we headed north, the sunshine allowed us to lower the Z3's soft-top; but as lorry after lorry slowed our progress on the main road, we decided to escape the fumes and Mrs T's Amazing Map-Reading Skills were called into play once more. Suckers for animal welfare, we couldn't resist the handmade signs that pointed the way to Hedgehog Care at Authorpe. In a chaotic house full of boxes and old clothes, Elaine Drewery has devoted her life to the care of sick hedgehogs. Blind, lame or victims of road accidents or strimmers, to Elaine they are all God's creatures who deserve a second chance. Mrs T adopted her gooey-eyed puppy look when asked if she would like to hold a baby hedgehog. "This one's being treated for ringworm," Elaine explained and I decided it was time to go.

"They think I'm mad," she said, as we made our donation and turned to leave. She may well be, but she'll definitely go to heaven where, hopefully, there will be fewer flies.

Our route took us on through Muckton, a tiny, quiet village — though I once read an obituary in the *Louth Standard* of a farmworker who had tired of the humdrum of living in Muckton Bottom and left at 14 years of age to seek fame and fortune in Muckton, two miles down the road!

It was at the *Standard* that I had begun my journalistic career, swapping A-level studies at grammar school in Grimsby for the country life of a cub reporter. But Louth was wasted on a 16-year-old, I realised as we pulled into the centre of what is surely one of England's most attractive Georgian market towns. Then, I had eschewed the beautiful old black-and-white Wheatsheaf Inn in Westgate ("bar for old fuddy-duddies") and preferred instead the dark and dingy passage that housed the equally dark and dingy Golden Fleece, with its ultra-loud juke box and customers with hair as long as my own. And not for me the beautiful Hubbard's Hills park which surrounds the fast-flowing River Lud ("all trees and grass") or the magnificent St James Church of cathedral-like proportions with a 295-foot spire ("full of God-botherers").

They say "use it or lose it" and it certainly proved true of the *Louth Standard*. It went into such decline it was seen off by a younger freesheet rival, the *Louth Leader,* which at least had the decency to become a paid-for paper again when it had the territory all to itself. The Standard offices in Cornmarket, where I had wrestled with the mysteries of the telephone (just one between four reporters) and the typewriter ("hit the keys hard or sub-editors can't read the carbon copy"), are now a café where we stopped off for refreshments. At least it wasn't my turn to make the tea.

The Blue Stone Inn where Byng stayed is no more, either, knocked down in 1912. Named after a giant boulder that had been deposited by a glacier during the Ice Age, the inn stood at the corner of Upgate and Mercer Row. It was demolished for road-widening and the stone repositioned outside the town's museum. The inn had been the chosen setting in 1761 for the inhabitants of Louth to drink the health of the newly-crowned "mad" King George III. Thirty years later, Byng was unimpressed: *'We supp'd hastily, at ten o'clock, and were in our beds, shabby things in shabby rooms, by eleven o'clock. This is a mean, dirty ill-managed inn; for the master is dead and no woman is competent of such a charge.'* Thank goodness he didn't live to see women get the vote.

The ladies of the town had celebrated the coronation at the Mansion House in Upgate, called the *'Assembly and Card Rooms'* by Byng and described as *'elegant'*. The building later became the Mechanics' Institute.

Byng also visited the shop of Mr Adam Eve, where he bought some of the Lincolnshire "stuff" — a coarse woollen fabric. The Eve name has survived as Eve and Ranshaw, proudly boasting service in the reigns of nine monarchs from George III to Elizabeth II. A splendid old-fashioned department store, a mini Harrods transposed to the Lincolnshire Wolds, it offers quality goods at reasonable prices with helpful staff who cut short their chat to serve or just offer advice. Could it catch on? We bought some stuff, too — stuff for our new bedroom back home — before continuing our day of nostalgia.

I can't think of holidays without imagining the Lincolnshire coast. As a child, it was never an option to go abroad, or even to Cornwall or Wales. The Good Lord had provided miles and miles of golden sand less than an hour's drive from our front door so my brother and sister and I went mostly to Mablethorpe, first by train then later by borrowed car. We always stayed in a caravan and if there weren't enough beds then I, as the youngest, would find myself on the suitcases.

But once, when my siblings considered themselves too old and too sophisticated to go on holiday with Mum and Dad, we ended up at Saltfleet. Not only did I have a bed of my own but a whole room. I was allowed to wander around the caravan site unaccompanied and remember winning a racquet at the camp bingo hall then confidently going back to win another so I could play tennis with Mum.

And "provided I behaved myself" I was also allowed in the village pub — the New Inn — to sip my cherryade alongside the pint-swilling holidaymakers and the sceptical locals. I thought I was the bee's knees.

Byng lunched on cheese at the Old Inn after a ride along the sands from Theddlethorpe, *'the widest I ever rode upon. This is a poor place under the sea bank with a wretched inn-bathing house. Nothing but the sea view to support us'.*

Happily, the Old and New Inns turned out to be one and the same, having been renamed early in 1800 after building extensions and a change of image from "a place frequented by the gentry in the summer season for the eating of fish" to a centre for "sea bathing for travellers from the midland counties of Nottingham and Leicester".

The beautiful gabled brick building, three storeys high, is out of all proportion to the size of the village. But it reflects Saltfleet's history, first as a thriving market town and port with a prosperous trade in fish, salt and agricultural products, then, after the river silted up, as a bathing resort. Smugglers throughout history found the inn a handy stopping-off point as they traded wool for brandy and tobacco.

Two projecting bow windows at the rear, which once overlooked the sea, now give on to a giant caravan site. It is as a social club serving the site that the New Inn manages to survive, its letting rooms and 100-seat dining room having long since closed. Meals are served only at weekends, but it is a miracle the building has survived at all. If it were in the south of England, it would undoubtedly have been converted to a 'boutique hotel' or at the very least a 'gastro-pub' called the Smugglers or the Salt Cellar and would attract a very different clientele.

A stormy north wind confronted Byng as he made his way through the villages of Marshchapel, Tetney and Humberston, first with Colonel Bertie — *'he has purchased a pair of small tight-moulded foreign horses with a curricle in which my heavy baggage will be placed'* — then on his own horse again *'upon the Sands to Cleathorps Inn, a bathing place of a better complexion than the two others we have seen upon this coast. We desired privacy and procured a dirty little parlour with a fire, for it was dismally cold; At last did we get some tolerable victuals to eat and we sat muddling over the fire'.*

No such luck for the Taylors who found the doors of the Dolphin Inn, built on the same site in the 1820s, firmly bolted at lunchtime. We both had memories of the Dolphin at the heart of Cleethorpes life, bustling with tourists, day-trippers and locals; a journalists' watering hole where we interviewed the 'big' stars (the Nolan Sisters, Lonnie Donegan) and the not-so-big (Skeletons Alive, the Singing Chickens) of the summer season on Cleethorpes Pier.

We retired across the road to O'Neills Irish pub, where the friendly barman informed us the Dolphin now preferred nocturnal customers of more tender years than our own. So I must leave the last word on the place to my elder brother, who bravely went to watch his son playing in a band there and remembers: "My shoes were sticking to the beer-sodden carpet as a young girl wearing a dress no bigger than a curtain pelmet was bustled past me, effing and blinding, by two mean-looking bouncers en route for the exit." At least Byng found the people *'civil and the bill reasonable'* at *'the best of the Lincolnshire bathing shops'*.

The New Inn at Great Limber looks older but it did not open its doors until 1818 and so was not the ale house where Byng took his noonday stop on the 12th of July 1791: *'At early noon, we came to Gt Limbe, near to which Mr Pelham in his grounds is erecting a mausoleum (a little Ratcliffe library) of which Mr Wyatt, the famous architect, gives the plan and directs the execution. Below it, for the sake of contrast and miserable comparison, stands (for the reception of the living) an alehouse so bad as not even to afford cheese! We did get a slice of baked beef, not to be eaten (beer and bread as bad) and a glass of brandy and water.'*

My mother had the same experience with the beef at the New Inn when we took her for Sunday lunch while researching our tour. After we ordered, our own vegetarian lasagne arrived so quickly from a small kitchen at the side of the dining room that we wondered if Paul Daniels had been appointed head chef. Mum asked for a doggy bag and we politely left to look at a row of three old cottages near the church which may have been the site of Byng's alehouse. Great Limber, now as then, is owned by the Earl of Yarborough. The village was probably founded by monks who built the church and, it is rumoured, a monastery behind. Wherever there were abbots, there was hospitality and alehouses flourished.

Of the more than 120 abbeys and priories that were once in Lincolnshire, few survive. The most impressive is at Thornton, where we called as a delaying tactic on our reluctant route to Barton. Colonised from Kirkham Priory in North Yorkshire, the Augustinian house at Thornton was founded in 1139 by William le Gros. Less than 10 years later it was raised to the status of an abbey.

Dissolved in 1539, it was held under the guardianship of the last prior for the next two years before being re-founded by Henry VIII as a college of secular canons. The new house lasted for just six years and after its dissolution the site was granted to the Bishop of Lincoln. An early 19th-century excavation was carried out before the site was put in the care of English Heritage.

The red-brick gatehouse was built at the end of the 14th century and stands defiant, almost intact. Byng thought *'Thurnton-College'* and Lincoln Cathedral the two grand features of the county.

And so to Barton as the heavens opened. There are so many well-preserved houses and so little new development that Barton is probably one of the most attractive towns in Lincolnshire — almost a living museum. Unfortunately, a section of the local population is not so quaint or well-preserved. When we entered the George Hotel it was 'happy hour'. It had been our intention to eat wherever Byng had eaten and drink wherever he drank. Apologies, dear reader, but a quick glance into the bar of the George and our resolve just melted away. Pint-swilling, tattooed revellers filled the smoky room with their vulgar shouts. And some of the men looked none too savoury either.

We studied the menu in the window outside to see if there was anything we could possibly tackle.

"What about scampi* and chips?" I asked.

"A menu with footnotes." Mrs T was dubious. "What is *?"

I looked down, squinting. "*Made with reformed scampi. Or there's chicken* Kiev made from reformed chicken. All main meals £2.99."

"They might be reformed but I'm not prepared to give them a second chance and, besides, there's a nice-looking

Italian restaurant just down the road." I weakened. We had a great night — until it was time to return to our room.

My gran had in her bathroom a novelty bath mat which never failed to amuse me. On the plain green towelling were embroidered in black cotton two dirty feet marks. I was reminded of this as we studied our dingy en suite at the George, devoid of toiletries and with tiles missing from the wall. Yes, the same feet marks — except this was no embroidery. The carpet in the bedroom was stained, the sheets on our bed full of holes; some from wear, others from cigarette burns.

Byng always travelled with his own sheets. For the first time, we were jealous of his arrangements. But we had brought two towels which we laid on the bed before lying fully clothed to listen to the night's entertainment. The noise from the pub disco was awesome — we locked our door and hoped for sleep. Alas, the window would not close and, as the night wore on, the sounds from the streets reached a crescendo. Swearing, shouting, vomiting, urinating. Just another Friday night in Barton. Sad, really, because the Victorian architecture of the town is impressive, as is the view of the Humber Bridge, the longest single-span bridge in the world when it opened in 1981. There are art galleries and gift shops that hint at a more tranquil, bohemian way of life and pleasant walks by the river past the former Waterside Inn, where Byng wished he had stayed.

Next morning, tired and irritable, we ordered breakfast but couldn't face it. We interrupted a lady clearing up the night's debris to ask if we could pay. She switched off her vacuum cleaner and moved aside the biggest pile of cigarette ash I have ever seen in my life to place our bill on the counter and receive an ill-deserved £50 in cash.

'Most glad to part from Barton.' Ride on...

16ᴛʜ Jᴜʟʏ 1791 *Grantham spire would appear wonderfully if we had not lately seen that of Louth, so much more beautiful. The Angel Inn at Grantham bears a most venerable front, with an angel croun'd in stone on the top. We occupied a very old room but there are large ranges of buildings and of stabling behind. Our evening stroule was around the newly-built cross in the market place; to survey the George, a great, staring new inn; and, as the emptier, had been the better for us. My letters took up much time in reading and answering, till our supper came which, with the wine, were very tolerable.*

Bill for 1 night: 12s 0d *We went before breakfast to see old Draper in the stable. He has been run for 3 years as a post horse; and every year, having been put into training, has won a fifty pound plate.*

Angels and devils

Brigg — Spital — Gainsborough — Ancaster — Grantham

I t was good to leave Barton behind, return the hire car to Humberside Airport, pick up the BMW sports again and head for Brigg with the sun on our backs. Byng was kind to *'Glandford Bridge'* and enjoyed his stay at The Angel in Brigg market place. Supper on 13th July 1791 was *'well serv'd, the best we have had, as likewise our Oporto of which we finish'd the bottle'.*

The best he could hope for nowadays would be advice from his local council, as the inn was converted to municipal offices as part of the renovation of the town centre. The façade has been preserved and so has the interior glazed courtyard that was once a favourite meeting place for farmers. The refurbished ballroom acts as a community centre to make up for demolition of the neighbouring Corn Exchange.

Outside, he would be able to enjoy a magnificent Sargent's ice cream and watch folk musicians playing in the bandstand. With the help of funding, Brigg has fought against decay and is working hard to make itself an attractive tourist stop. Fayres, farmers' markets and arts festivals have all brought the town centre to life and encouraged small shops run by local people with a commitment to customer care.

Mrs T couldn't resist a peek at the site of her old school, Brigg Convent. A strict Catholic education has left her with two legacies. She's a complete atheist but a whiz at Bible questions on pub quiz night. The nuns have long departed and there's just a housing development where once young girls were encouraged to learn the skills that would make them 'the perfect wives for local businessmen'.

I wouldn't want to live in Spital — Spital-in-the-Street to give it its full name. And it's not just the embarrassment of having to tell people your address. The street in question is Ermine Street, the lonely Roman road that linked Lincoln to the Humber crossing at Winteringham in the north of the county. And the hamlet's curious name comes from a hospital founded there as a refuge for travellers in the 12th century. No, I could live with the jokes. I just couldn't live with the traffic which thunders past on what is now the A15, a racetrack for heavy goods vehicles and daredevil motorists who like to pull out and drive at you on your side of the white line. The buildings are just inches away from the kerb and crossing the road should be attempted only by the very nimble with plenty of time on their hands. There's no shop and no pub since the Moncks Arms at nearby Caenby Corner closed its doors and fell prey to vandals.

Byng paid 12 shillings and fourpence for a night in Spital but noted that, even in 1791, *'the greater part of this inn is old and shattered. Yet there are some additional parlours and bedrooms with tolerable stabling, opposite two chapel-like buildings'*. With so little to go on, we weren't hopeful of finding any traces. But in the interminable wait to cross, we were forced to look away from the swirling wind and dust kicked up by lorries and struck gold. Apparently, until late in the 17th century, the quarter sessions for the Kirton division of Lindsey were held at Spital's old chapel. A new one was built in 1661 and is maintained to this day, opening to pilgrims several times a year. Unfortunately the chapel's wall had recently been toppled by a wayward lorry. Would the driver have been more careful if he had understood the building's Latin inscription? "He who destroys this temple, may God destroy him."

We learned much of this information from the tenant of a farmhouse opposite who came out to ask why we were taking photos of her home. "No offence but we get a lot of gypsies round here." The offence offer was difficult to refuse but I bit my tongue, explained our mission and said her house looked a little like it could have been an inn.

"Oh yes, some of the people who come to look after the chapel still call it The Ostrich. It's called Cromwell House now as it's recorded that he stayed here. Dick Turpin, too, they say, but there's no real proof."

Convinced of our genuineness, she invited us to look round the back of the building where the tops of the cellar arches were still visible. In the garden, there are signs of other outbuildings associated with an inn but a barn cuts unsympathetically through the plot. "It's a lovely house if you like cold," she sighed.

There have to be ugly towns, otherwise how would we recognise a beautiful one? Towns without character, without style, almost without hope. So Gainsborough performs a valuable function. With its drab Victorian buildings and air of Dickensian poverty, it could probably have re-invented itself as a film set for gritty northern dramas had Tesco not built a hideous modern supermarket, with all the charm of a high-security jail, bang in the middle of it all.

But even the blackest of clouds has a silver lining and in the midst of all this drabness stands Gainsborough Old Hall, a Tudor masterpiece. Formerly the home of the Hickman family, it became a linen factory, a theatre, a pub, a chapel and much more before the Friends of the Old Hall Association set about its restoration in 1952. It is now run by the county council and is open to the public.

We parked the BMW in a street just out of town, by boarded-up shops and a second-hand car emporium and looked at each other knowingly. "I'll stay with the car," said Mrs T, locking the doors from inside. "You go find the Blackamoor's Head." But I knew I wouldn't. Even Byng knew I wouldn't: *'A mean, dirty inn in the market place. A better inn, now that the new stone bridge over the Trent is built, must be open'd.'*

Surprisingly, the inn did survive until 1960, having changed its name to the Black Head in a bid to attract more customers. Okay, so not the public relations masterstroke of the 20th century. And, yes, we did all the jokes about it being a squeeze in the bar and customers arriving by acne carriage. At first, Gainsborough Library thought the inn had occupied the magnificent old building that now belongs to HSBC bank. But further research revealed it was on the site of the Sixties nonentity built and run by the Co-op.

The sun was shining and the Saturday market in full swing as I took my photos and made my way back to a nervous Mrs T. There was even a scene from *Romeo and Juliet* being performed by young actors from the Lincoln Shakespeare Company to promote their summer tour. Unlike them, I had more will to go than care to stay.

From Gainsborough, Byng headed back to his beloved Rein Deer at Lincoln for a *'well dress'd supper of tripe and lamb's fry'*. Mmmmm! On the way he stopped *'at the side of the canal leading to Lincoln at a clean looking public house called Daventers-Nook where we water'd our cattle and drank some liquor'*.

Research had proved unhelpful and we held out little

hope of tracking down this particular watering hole. But, as we passed alongside the Foss Dyke canal, an office building caught our eye. "Does that look like an old inn to you?" I asked, idly wondering if an ability to spot a pub at great distance would be worth adding to my CV. "Yes, and the village is called Drinsey Nook," said the Map-Reader-In-Chief.

Coincidence enough. We turned off and found, in the old stables behind the house, an artisan making model tugs. I have to admit that, at the start of my journalistic career, I wasn't the best news reporter in the world. I was far too shy to ask the difficult question, too thin-skinned to take rejection and bounce back. My virgin foot rarely made it past the front gate, let alone into the door jamb. But I compensated by becoming king of the off-beat human interest feature. I could listen and observe where others preferred to interrogate.

So my past life flashed before me as I started to question my new victim. Unusual Hobbies Number 73 — Model Tug Making: "Sorry to bother you. Do you know if the old house was ever a pub?"

"I've lived here all my life and I've only known it as a house and then a garage," he mused, ceaselessly filing a tiny brass piston. "Because it's on the road and the canal, it was a very popular stop-off for cars and boats refuelling." More filing. "Come to think of it, though, they do say that it was once a pub and that when the Italian prisoners of war were here they spent so much time in there it was closed down by the authorities. That would be around 1948."

Jeremy Paxman eat your heart out. "That would explain the stables then — if it was an inn? But not why it was called Daventers-Nook. Perhaps that was just a mistake by the author."

"It's only been called Drinsey Nook since the 1800s; it

was something different before then."

Game, set and match. John Taylor, please come up and collect your Journalist of the Year Award...

The Red Arrows aerobatic team performed a fly-past as we skirted Lincoln and headed for Ancaster. A poster revealed that, after our personal tribute, they were due at Waddington Air Show.

With a history that goes back to the Romans and a number of fine buildings, Ancaster should be a memorable village. Not for Byng: *'a poor village where we got some good chops and were quiet'* was all he could remember about the Red Lion. Built on either side of Ermine Street, Ancaster seems to have no real heart. There is much evidence of excavations but, like a child playing with his toys, it's as if no one has bothered to put everything back in its proper place. The Red Lion is mentioned in Kelly's directories as late as 1905 and a map of that year puts it alongside the Oddfellows Hall. There is just a gap there now giving access to the fields behind. Like Byng, we were *'glad to hasten away from this miserable country'* and head for our night stop at Grantham.

Over recent years, planners have set about the destruction of Grantham town centre with a vengeance. Beautiful buildings have been torn down to make way for concrete office blocks, car parks and traffic systems.

Thankfully, the jewel in the crown has been left to sparkle. Quite simply one of the oldest and most important historic inns in England, the Angel & Royal has been welcoming visitors for 800 years. Called the Angel until 1866, the inn started life as a hostel for the Knights Templar who owned the land on which it stands and took rent to support their work at nearby Temple Bruer.

A visit in the 12th century by Edward III and Queen Phillippa of Hainault was marked by the installation over the grand archway of a stone angel carrying a crown. King John held court there two years before the signing of the Magna Carta and in 1483 Richard III stayed in the state room, the Chambre du Roi.

Charles I in 1633 and later George IV lent their patronage, too, but it wasn't until a visit by the Prince of Wales, later Edward VII, that the inn changed its name to the Angel & Royal. Rumour has it that 'Royal Angel' was vetoed, as the fun-loving future king was anything but.

In Byng's day the Angel was at the peak of its success, serving the mail coaches which travelled between London and York and on to Edinburgh and Aberdeen. Only the advent of the railway in the early 19th century would change all that.

After the last war, the business was bought by Forte Hotels — if there are three words which strike terror into the heart of a true *bon viveur* they have to be 'Trust House Forte' — and in recent years there has been a succession of owners, including several brewery companies. The Angel & Royal's revival started in 2002 when a group of local businessmen bought the hotel and decided to restore it to its former glories.

Our bedroom was small but very well equipped and we eagerly sought a drink in the famous Angel Bar, reopened after five years of decay. The room is dominated by a huge fireplace, nine feet wide and six feet high, which was not discovered until 1947 when workmen were removing plaster. Word of the improvements to the Angel had obviously spread like wildfire and there was quite a crush as we pushed our way through to the last vacant window seat to enjoy champagne by the glass, poured by a jovial barman who polished the flutes as he chatted.

With its stone walls and open fire, the King's Room Restaurant is very little changed from when King Richard signed the death warrant for the rebellious Duke of Buckingham. But we were told we should have specifically requested a table when we made our reservation and would have to eat in the modern downstairs bistro. A chat with the manager and an explanation of our mission, followed by another glass of bubbly, and we were soon accommodated in a secluded corner of the magnificent chamber while he explained other ambitious plans for his hotel, including a ladies-only lounge for women travelling on their own.

An excellent dinner of smoked salmon, prawn and avocado and smoked macaroni cheese for Mrs T with brie tartelet and roasted salmon for me was a bargain at £30, as was a bottle of Taittinger rosé at £35 — all served by mature, competent and helpful staff. With a room rate of £105, this was not the cheapest but without doubt the most enjoyable stay of the Tour so far.

Our evening stroll took us to the old George Hotel, praised by Charles Dickens as one of the great coaching inns. The façade survives but behind is a 50,000 sq ft shopping mall opened in 1992. At the market cross, the streets were filling with the now-familiar scantily-clad girls and foul-mouthed, out-of-control youths. Every bar had bouncers on the doors and obscenities filled the air. To our terror (it was only 10.30 at night), one group of youngsters climbed onto a car which had pulled up at red lights and began to trash it, kicking in the roof and windscreen. Why fight terrorism around the world when urban terrorism is on view on every English town street at the weekend? How can an enterprise like the Angel & Royal be expected to thrive when it is not safe to venture out? And we wonder why American tourists are in short supply.

It is obviously in the interests of big business that

everyone drinks more than he can handle. And what if there is damage — so long as it's not on our premises?

Cheap gin, first imported from the Netherlands in the 1690s, became an extremely popular drink in the early 18th century. Politicians and religious leaders argued that gin drinking encouraged laziness and criminal behaviour. In 1729 Parliament increased the tax and this led to complaints, culminating in the 1743 Gin Riots. The government responded by reducing duties and penalties, claiming that moderate measures would be easier to enforce. How familiar does that sound?

A previous landlord of the Angel, a Mr Solomon, made a bequest in his will of 1706 to provide 40 shillings a year for a sermon to be preached every October in Grantham church "wherein the subject shall be chiefly against drunkenness, that sin being the inlet of almost all others". The wisdom of Solomon — still unheeded after 300 years of 'progress'.

The George, Stamford

17ᴛʜ Jᴜʟʏ 1791 *We spread all our canvas as to reach Stamford (just as the storm fell) and shelter in the gateway of the George Inn; when, finding the storm to continue, we order'd beds and supper at this nasty, hot town inn, so unlike the coolness and cleanliness of Wansford-Bridge to which we intended. The Coll continued to Burleigh House to make his enquiries after the Earl of Exeter.*

Bill for 1 night: 13s 9d *The march of the allies has continued one fortnight and we have done enough. I have observed upon most of the county and the Coll has seen all the family ruins, monuments &c &c. We now divided the 3 last shillings of the stock-purse. Parting is always a melancholy time. So much of time and of money gone!*

Thus ended the conjunct Lincolnshire tour.

Bertie and George

Greetham — Stamford

Colonel Albemarle Peregrine Bertie (pronounced Bartie) 1744-1818, ninth Earl of Lindsey, was a soldier, Member of Parliament for Boston and Stamford, cousin of the Duke of Ancaster and a positive pain in the backside, according to his friend and travelling companion John Byng.

Bertie (Bartie, remember, like arty and farty) served in the 1st Foot Guards with Byng and accompanied him on his Ride Into Oxfordshire and Warwickshire in 1785 and his Tour Into Kent in 1790.

'From old acquaintance and frequent travelling with Col B, we are become accustom'd to each other's modes and long familiarity breeds conversation.'

But it also breeds contempt and many of Bertie's little ways were guaranteed to annoy. Byng preferred to ride on horseback, *'my night cap in my own pocket'*, and blend in with the crowds at the inns where he stayed. Bertie was a snob and a social climber and always travelled with heaps of baggage in some kind of horse-drawn carriage.

'The Colonel is not so well form'd for a traveller as I am,' records Byng gloomily at the George in Barton. *'He moves in state; trunks laden with dressing apparatus, with snuff, with books, from Shakespeare down to a Court calendar!'*

Bertie spent much of the time complaining — about the smell of tobacco or feathers or of bugs biting. And he liked to hail his servant to the dinner table to pass him the salt, even when it was within reaching distance, much to Byng's annoyance and embarrassment.

Many of Lincolnshire's churches contain monuments to various branches of the Bertie family. It seems Albemarle was related to most of the county's worthies — including the Willoughbys and Eresbys and the great Duke of Ancaster at Lincolnshire's grandest seat, Grimsthorpe Castle — and he used the 1791 Tour to look up his relatives and their magnificent properties and to try to ingratiate himself.

Bertie's brown-nosing eventually paid off when he inherited the title Earl of Lindsey and, with it, the magnificent Uffington Hall just outside Stamford. *'He has long been climbing in hope to grandeur, to a post coach and to pompous espousals. And now they are come!! To my surprise — and almost, I may think to his own,'* wrote Byng some three years later.

The two old soldiers' friendship of 32 years came to an end when, on his Tour Into Bedfordshire in 1794, Byng was passed on a Lincolnshire road by the now-General Bertie and his *'vain, weak, proud, cold and quick temper'd'* wife. They exchanged pleasantries but no invitation was forthcoming to the Bertie country seat, Byng not being considered wealthy enough to count among their social set.

Though the two men later met occasionally, Byng remarked: *'He and I have lost all conversation. He has buried memory in pomp and new methods and is struggling forth to grandeur: I stare and smile at him and shrink into my own snugness.'*

Uffington Hall was burnt down in 1904 but two sets of imposing gates, leading to nowhere, still decorate the village. The main gates, fully restored, stand between two stone lodges. Opposite the church, another pair reveal a garden walk of yew trees behind.

The family name lives on in Uffington's Bertie Lane, where stands Ye Olde Bertie Arms, now pronounced 'Berty' by the chef who was not able to serve us cheese sandwiches, only "Cheddar-filled baguettes". As one pretension dies, another takes its place.

Byng's own lunch had been taken at the Royal Oak at Greetham, then as now in the county of Rutland. Though the village still boasts some beautiful pubs, the Royal Oak closed its doors in the 1920s. It is now known as Oak House and is a residential care home for the elderly. It no longer looks like an inn but a marvellous place to spend one's final years. A bridge in the grounds crosses the village stream and a resident waved to us as she watched two ducks preening themselves on the banks.

Our final destination, like Byng's, was the George of Stamford — not so much a hotel as an institution, in the best possible sense. It once belonged to the Abbots of Crowland so there has probably been an inn on the site for more than a thousand years. It grew from a tiny stopping-off place for the Knights of Saint John, en route to Jerusalem, to a huge establishment, taking over the religious buildings on either side.

The main block of the George was rebuilt by Lord Burghley in 1597 and a new façade and the famous gallows sign straddling the main road were added in the 18th century to take advantage of the increase in coach traffic. In Byng's time, 40 coaches a day passed through Stamford — 20 up and 20 down — and, as you enter the George, there are still two doors marked London and York, former waiting rooms for passengers who assembled there as the coaches changed horses in the stable-yard.

If location, location and location really are the three main assets for a hotel, then the George is ideally placed, situated as it is on the Great North Road and in the centre of England. Many must be the lovers who have stolen a secret night here and many the businessmen who have been hired or fired in one of the wood-panelled private rooms.

Just one of 400 listed buildings in the magnificent stone town of Stamford, where *Middlemarch* was filmed for the BBC, the George is a rabbit warren of stairs and rooms and more stairs and more rooms and it is easy to get lost without help. Fortunately, there are plenty of staff to point the bemused traveller in the right direction. There was even a porter — the first time on our tour — to help with the bags as we made our way through the sunny courtyard, still packed with Sunday diners at five o'clock in the evening.

Charles I spent his last night as a free man here in 1645. And it was here that our own Lincolnshire odyssey was to end after just eight short days. When we checked in, we were wished a happy 20th wedding anniversary and told we had been upgraded. A card was waiting in our room — a huge suite with canopied bed, two large wardrobes and a sitting area with the cutest of window seats overlooking a private walled garden.

And here, at last, were books — half a dozen in the room and, in reception, a bookcase full of second-hand volumes for sale in aid of charity.

There is much to praise about the George, thoughtful touches like a trouser press and a clothes brush in the wardrobe. Beds are turned down at night; your early morning call comes not from a machine but from a knock at the door as tea and freshly-squeezed orange juice are brought to your bedside.

Friends who were also celebrating their 20th anniversary joined us for dinner in the elegant dining room, where jacket and tie were insisted upon. Food was of a high quality — asparagus and salmon with bubble and squeak for Mrs T; a trio of vegetarian dishes for me.

The hotel offered a "Serene Sunday" rate of £70 room and breakfasts for the Sabbath. But the staff, obviously still hyper after a nerve-racking lunchtime marathon, seemed unable or unwilling to switch into serenity mode. When we hadn't made our choice from the menu in the allotted time, we were left to stew. At the table, we were each made to recite our complete order so that relevant cutlery could be laid out before us. We were constantly asked which were our wine and which our water glasses, testing us to see if we were paying attention. And, most annoying of all, we were asked if everything was okay before a fork had even reached our mouths.

Mrs T likened it to being waited on by sheepdogs — a little nip here, a little bark there to chivvy everything along and keep everyone in his place. Our second bottle of Chablis was warm and when we declined dessert on the grounds that the choice was rather predictable — summer pudding, tiramisu, crème caramel — we were chided with "so I've brought the sweet trolley all the way over here for nothing, then?".

The George is probably a victim of its own success — there is now a row of up-market shops, a bistro, a restaurant, conferences, exhibitions — and you can't help but feel that the "business" of the hotel takes precedence over the wishes and needs of the individual guest. Here a trainee is checking the bottle store, in reception the noise of a vacuum cleaner drowns out conversation; in the garden room at breakfast a girl on work experience is indoctrinated with page one of the training manual just feet away from us.

But, despite all that, we agreed the George was the only inn where we wished we were staying another night —

though this time we would probably have eaten at Pizza Express across the road.

Mrs T voted the next morning's breakfast of smoked salmon and scrambled egg the highlight of the week. There were many more local accents to be heard and a certain serenity had been restored. Plenty of help with our bags and good wishes for a safe journey home made us sorry that the Tour had come to an end and reluctant to leave behind our native Lincolnshire. A torrential downpour which lasted all the way to France helped overcome the regret...

The Bull Hotel, Horncastle

*I enjoy each Tour three times over; viz,
by anticipation, by the present enjoyment,
and by a record of the past.*

80

Present enjoyment

The night after we left Stamford we were back in France at a small hotel south of Calais. It was refreshing to eat smaller portions of well-cooked fresh food; to discuss the menu in detail with someone who actually cared that you enjoyed your stay and to see contented dogs at the feet of their masters in the dining room. England and France share so much history they must once have shared a love of food, a joy in serving, an interest in their customers. When did the English lose it?

On this tour, we came near to contentment. The White Hart at Spilsby offered what it has offered for hundreds of years: civility, cleanliness, good food and a comfy bed, all at a reasonable price. At extra cost, the Angel & Royal at Grantham added a little sophistication. In Sempringham, we experienced what no amount of riches can buy in Monaco — silence.

Lincolnshire's charm is as the "forgotten county". Sadly, thanks to newspapers, TV programmes about relocation and ridiculously high property prices in the south, it is forgotten no more. The countryside is as beautiful as ever — particularly in the Wolds — and there is much to delight the eye: old churches, old manor houses and, yes, old inns. But there are too many bungalows, too much traffic and too many weekend drunks in most of the market towns.

On a return visit in 2005, what has changed? The Red

Cow at Donington still stands forlornly empty. So, too, does the Greyhound at Folkingham, where a fire "believed to have been started by a squatter" destroyed ancient oak timbers. Part of the roof had caved in before firefighters could bring the blaze under control.

The White Hart at Spalding has reopened though, disappointingly, not under that name as the planners had hoped. One half is now an inviting Chinese restaurant, the Shanghai Garden; the other a neon and plastic establishment called Shooters Bar. The outbuildings have been converted to offices for a firm of accountants and a gift shop, the Teddy Bears' Cottage.

And, happily, the builders did finish their protracted work at the Bull at Horncastle. We enjoyed a drink in front of a blazing fire as the old folk of the town stampeded into the restaurant for a pensioners' special lunch. The bedrooms are open for business and the Bull is earning a reputation as a live music venue.

We went back to the Angel & Royal at Grantham to celebrate my birthday and made two unsuccessful attempts at ordering an edible vegetarian meal. Much of the optimism and excitement we had found when the inn reopened had evaporated. The barman bemoaned his lot as we drank our complimentary wine and at breakfast the eggs were watery and the anaemic mushrooms straight from the microwave.

Byng concluded: '*In Lincolnshire, a very large county, there is little for curiosity; but few gentlemen's seats and the sea-coast is flat and unpleasant. The two grand features of the county are the cathedral and Thurnton-College. Being of little travell, the inns are bad. The county is of a very sombre cast; the pleasantest parts are about Gainsborough, Spilsby and towards Bulingbroke*'.

The inns are still mostly bad and their binge-drinking young customers worse. Old Bolingbroke remains a gem of a

Wolds village, dominated by the ruins of Bolingbroke Castle where Henry IV was born in 1366, though they do say there are so many newcomers to the area that the pub on a Saturday night is reminiscent of *EastEnders'* Queen Vic.

For me, the best parts of the county are Stamford, an architectural gem, and Louth, the perfect Georgian market town. Tucked inside Byng's diaries, I found a poem written in 1786 by Richard Salmon, whose views still ring true:

Happy Louth

Indulgent Heaven on this much favour'd Town,
Has kindly pour'd its richest Blessings down;
Good Milk, good Bread, and wholesome home-brewed Ale;
Fine Springs of Water never known to fail;
Our Markets well supply'd with Flesh and Fish;
Here's all that Man can want, or Heart can wish.

And though the coast of Lincolnshire is very flat, it boasts miles and miles of empty sand where a dog can run and run until it is exhausted. We know. When we were disappointed on our first night at Folkingham, we headed for the sea — and that's where we bought our house!

BIBLIOGRAPHY

The Torrington Diaries by John Byng, edited by C. Bruyn Andrews and abridged by Fanny Andrews; Eyre & Spottiswoode, London 1954.

Rides Round Britain by John Byng, edited by Donald Adamson; The Folio Society, London 1996.

The Book of the Lincolnshire Seaside by David N. Robinson; Baron, Buckingham 1989.

The Book of Louth by David N. Robinson; Baron, 1992.

The Buildings of England: Lincolnshire by Nikolaus Pevsner and John Harris, revised by Nicholas Antram; Yale University Press, New Haven and London 2002.

Lincolnshire Houses by Henry Thorold; Michael Russell, Norwich 1999.

Lincolnshire in History and Lincolnshire Worthies by J. Medcalf; Ward, Lock & Co, London 1903.

I am indebted also to the hundreds of websites which record Lincolnshire happenings past and present and to the archives of *Lincolnshire Life* magazine, PO Box 81, Lincoln.